S 4

INTRODUCTION

When I began to work on this book my friends rallied round me in the most encouraging way. They dipped into the most treasured family collections of recipes, and the yellowed pages thus brought to light revealed the most exciting dishes from all parts of the world.

From the Far East I received some peculiarly worded recipes. One friend told me 'to wash a fish, then drip-dry it', another advised me 'to bathe a chicken in salt and then to squeeze it with flour'. However, they were all very useful and a great help in compiling this book. I spent many hours in the kitchen converting the different weights and measures, in particular the Oriental ones which recommend a 'thumbsize' or a 'fistful' of this or that and similar vague measures.

Wherever I can I have given the name of the dish as it is called in its own country, but have avoided naming it when I am not quite certain.

The reader will find in this book a large chapter on minced meat only, a subject hitherto much neglected which nevertheless provides great scope for varied and economical cookery.

It was an arduous but enjoyable task trying out the recipes for my book but I was glad to find that the results were much appreciated by my husband and our friends. I hope that my readers will find the same gratifying results when serving dishes selected from this book.

to individual taste. Each recipe in this book has the spices specified, but to simplify it, ready-made curry powder could be used in the amount of 1 dessertspoon of powder to 1 lb. of meat.

It is advisable to mix a little water or vinegar with curry powder to make it into a thick paste before using, or when grinding the spices, to sprinkle them with water or vinegar during the process.

Fenugreek: The seeds are used in preparing curries. Fenugreek is considered to help the digestion and often used in dishes for convalescents.

Garam masala (hot spices): These consist of equal amounts of cinnamon, cloves and cardamoms ground to a powder.

Garlic: Garlic is used in many European dishes and in every curry, but on account of its pungent and strong smell it should be used sparingly. When used for a curry, garlic is pounded together with other spices and then fried.

Ginger: Ginger is widely used in the East by Indians, Malayans and Chinese for cooking and also for medical purposes. In Europe powdered ginger is used for flavouring cakes and puddings. For Oriental cookery fresh ginger roots are used and they cannot be replaced by powdered ginger. The root should be peeled and then either chopped very finely or grated.

The Chinese make a delicious sweet by preserving fresh ginger roots in syrup.

Marjoram: An aromatic herb used where strong herbal flavour is called for. Never used in Oriental cookery.

Mint: A herb known and used in Europe and the East. Used widely for meat and vegetable dishes. Mint tea is considered a cure for indigestion.

Nutmeg: This is a dried fruit of a tree from the East Indies. The whole nut retains the flavour almost indefinitely and can be grated when needed. It has a very strong flavour and should be used sparingly.

Paprika: A mild kind of red pepper. Adds colour and flavour to a variety of meat and vegetable dishes.

Pepper: This is a universal spice used whole or ground in various European and Oriental meat dishes.

Water in which peppercorns have been boiled is considered in the East a remedy for indigestion.

Poppy seeds: Used in Europe for breads and cakes. In the East certain curries are made with poppy seeds in order to improve the flavour and to thicken the gravy. *Flour is never used for thickening gravies* in India or Malayan dishes.

Soya sauce: A liquid made from fermented soya beans and flour. This is used in almost every Chinese dish. For recipes in this book the *Gold Label Soya* is recommended.

Tamarind: The juice of tamarind is used in dishes requiring an acid flavour, in the way in which vinegar or lemon juice is used for European cooking. The tamarind fruit is steeped in water and all the fibres are removed. Then it is strained through a muslin bag or a strainer.

Thyme: A herb used in European cooking, mostly for meat dishes. Dried thyme intensifies in flavour with prolonged cooking and should be used in moderate quantities.

Turmeric: This is a root of the ginger family with a delicate aroma and a bright yellow colour. It is less known in Europe, but used widely in Oriental cookery. One teaspoon of powdered turmeric mixed with a beaten raw egg yolk is taken as a remedy for internal injuries and externally this powder is applied to wounds and bruises.

Ve-tsin (monosodium glutamate): This is a gourmet powder used in Chinese cooking. The powder is an extract of wheat flour that enhances the flavour of dishes to which it is added.

Wine: Wine is used in European and Chinese dishes. White and red wine are often used in the preparation of fish and meat in Europe, and a clear, yellow wine is used in Chinese cooking. Sherry can be substituted for the latter.

A FEW GENERAL NOTES

Quantities
Basically the recipes in this book are intended for four people but in some cases it will be apparent that they are sufficient for larger numbers.

When buying meat allow about 6 oz. per person of boneless meat and 8–10 oz. of meat with bones.

Flour
Plain flour should be used throughout this book unless otherwise stated.

Besan flour is made from gram dhal and can be bought from all Indian food stores.

Fat for frying
To clarify butter. Place the butter in a pan and heat it slowly. Remove the scum as it rises and when quite clear the butter is ready for use. Pour the butter into jars, being careful to leave the sediment in the pan.

Beef suet and vegetable fat. These are suitable for deep frying as they can be cleaned after use. To do this put the fat in a pan and add twice as much water as there is melted fat. Add one small peeled and sliced potato and bring to the boil. Simmer for about 15 minutes, then put it through a fine strainer and allow to set. Remove the solidified fat and discard the liquid.

SECTION ONE

Hors d'œuvre, Starters and Savouries

Many starters and hors d'œuvre also make suitable endings to a meal. It is for this reason that I have grouped cold and hot starters and savouries together in this book.

Cold dishes

Chicken mousse (*French*)
Cornets of smoked salmon
  (*Russian*)
Cucumber boats (*French*)
Herrings in sour cream (*Polish*)

Liver pâté (*Danish*)
Pig's foot jelly (*Polish*)
Shrimp cocktail (*Japanese*)
Stuffed eggs (*Swiss*)
Various salads

Hot dishes

Baba with herrings (*Polish*)
Bacon balls (*Danish*)
Cheese balls (*Danish*)
Cheese and bread pudding
  (*German*)
Cheese slices (*Austrian*)
Cheese croquettes (*Swiss*)
Cheese on skewers (*Swiss*)
Chicken shami kebabs (*Indian*)
Cottage cheese fritters (*Israeli*)
Croûtons with onions (*Polish*)
Eggs à la Suisse (*Swiss*)
Eggs akuri (*Parsee*)

Egg and aubergine (*Israeli*)
Eggs Imperial (*Austrian*)
Eggs Provençale (*French*)
Stuffed eggs (*Polish*)
Eggs surprise (*Polish*)
Green pea patties (*Parsee*)
Ham rolls (*Scandinavian*)
Ham rolls with cheese (*Swiss*)
Kofta curry (*Pakistani*)
Masala Dosai (*Indian*)
Onion tart (*French*)
Potato bliny (*Estonian*)
Salmon patties (*French*)

Semolina patties (*Indian*)

Stuffed tomatoes (*Italian*)

Stuffed tomatoes (*Israeli*)

Various pasta dishes

COLD DISHES

Chicken mousse : Mousse de pulard
(French)

2 cups boiled chicken (minced)	4 tablesp. thick cream
½ lemon (juice)	2 cups chicken stock
3–4 tablesp. mayonnaise	2 envelopes of powdered gelatine
salt and pepper	(1 oz.)

Mix the minced chicken with lemon juice and mayonnaise and season with salt and pepper. Fold in the thick cream.

Soften the gelatine in 2 tablespoons of cold chicken stock, add to the rest of the stock and dissolve over hot water. Cool, and when cold stir into the chicken mixture.

Rinse a ring mould (or any other mould) with cold water and pour in the chicken mixture. Chill until firm. Turn out on to a serving plate and fill the centre (if a ring mould was used) with lettuce leaves.

Cornets of smoked salmon
(Russian)

smoked salmon	raw lemon cut into wedges
black caviar	

Cut smoked salmon into small squares and shape into cornets. Fill the cornets with black caviar and place on a plate. Decorate with the lemon wedges.

Cucumber boats: Barquettes de concombres
(French)

4 small or 2 large cucumbers	1 teasp. lemon juice
8 oz. freshly cooked or tinned sal-	2 tablesp. mayonnaise
mon	salt and pepper
4 chopped gherkins	

To prepare the boats: Cut each cucumber into half, scoop out the centre, cut each half into pieces about 3 inches long and shape the ends of these pieces.

To prepare the filling: Flake the salmon and mix with the chopped gherkins, lemon juice and mayonnaise. Season to taste with salt and pepper.

Fill the cucumber boats with the salmon mixture and serve on a plate decorated with watercress, slices of hard-boiled egg and tomatoes.

Note: Lobster instead of salmon may be used for the filling.

Herrings in sour cream : Sledzie z smietanie
(*Polish*)

2 salted herrings	1 cup sour cream
1 small onion	salt, sugar, lemon juice
1 medium-sized apple	chopped parsley

Soak the herrings overnight. Skin and bone the soaked herrings, cut them into halves and then cut each half into 3 or 4 pieces. Place these on a dish. Pour the sauce over the herrings and sprinkle with chopped parsley for decoration.

To make the sauce: Chop the onion finely; coarsely grate the apple; put onion and apple into a bowl, then add salt, sugar and lemon juice to taste. Pour in sour cream and mix all ingredients together.

Liver pâté : Hjemmelavet leverpostej
(*Danish*)

1 lb. calf liver	2 teasp. salt
½ lb. pork fat	¼ teasp. pepper
2 oz. butter	sugar
2 oz. flour	1 beaten egg
½ pint milk	

Mince the liver and the pork fat twice. Make a white sauce with the butter, flour and milk and add the minced liver and pork fat to it. Season with salt and pepper and add a pinch of sugar and the beaten egg. Grease a long baking tin, and pour in the liver mixture. Bake in a slow oven (300° F., Gas reg. 2) for 1–1½ hours. Cool and when cold turn out of tin and cut into slices for serving.

Pig's foot jelly: Galaveta z nozek wieprzowch
(Polish)

1½ lb. pig's trotters	a few peppercorns
½ lb. lean pork (without bones)	salt
1 carrot	water
1 onion	lettuce leaves
1 stalk celery	slices of lemon
2 cloves garlic	
1 bay leaf	1 boiled carrot for decoration

Cut the trotters into pieces and place in a saucepan together with the meat, vegetables, garlic, bay leaf and peppercorns. Cover with cold water. Bring to the boil, then cover the saucepan and simmer very slowly until the meat will come off the bone (about 4 hours). Drain the meat and keep the stock. Cut the meat and return it to the saucepan together with the stock. Season with salt, bring to the boil and simmer for a minute or two; then remove from the heat. Rinse a mould in cold water. Place a carrot cut into fancy shapes in the bottom of the mould, then pour the meat and stock over this. Leave mould in a cold place to set. When the mould is set, turn it out on to a round dish and serve garnished with lettuce leaves and slices of lemon.

Shrimp cocktail: Shunomono
(Japanese)

1 large cucumber	1 teasp. sugar
20 shrimps (boiled and shelled)	lemon juice

Slice the cucumber very thinly, sprinkle with salt and leave for about 30 minutes. Place the shrimps in a bowl, add the sugar and lemon juice to taste, add the drained cucumber and mix well. Serve mixture in well-chilled individual bowls or glasses.

Stuffed eggs
(Swiss)

1 hard-boiled egg per person	salt
celery	pepper
parsley	mayonnaise
butter	

Cool the hard-boiled eggs under cold running water. Shell them and cut each egg into half (across the egg). Cut a small piece off the bottom of each half so that it will stand upright. Ease out the yolks, put them into a bowl and mash well. Add the finely chopped celery and very finely chopped parsley. Season with salt and pepper. Add a little softened butter and bind all together with mayonnaise. Fill the egg whites with the mixture, place on a plate and decorate.

Note: There are several ways one can decorate this dish. An unusual and attractive way is to cut a thin piece of salami, gather it together like a flower and push it into the centre of the stuffed egg. Put a sprig of parsley or watercress into the centre of the salami flower. Instead of salami any other suitable type of continental sausage could be used and asparagus tips or celery fringes could easily replace the parsley or watercress.

Various salads

Many salads make suitable starters and these recipes are given in Section Nine, but for convenience I list below the most obvious:

Aubergine salad	Herring and potato salad
Cheese salad	Green pepper salad
Fish salad	Celeriac salad

HOT DISHES

Baba with herrings: Babka z sledzi
(Polish)

2 salted herrings
4 medium-sized potatoes
1 beaten egg
milk

2 tablesp. sour cream
pepper
dried breadcrumbs

Soak the herrings in milk overnight, or longer if they are very salty. Remove the skin and bone, then mince the fish with the potatoes which have been boiled in their skins, allowed to go cold and then skinned. Stir in the beaten egg, the sour cream and the pepper. The herrings should be salty enough, but salt can be added to taste, if necessary. Grease a pudding or cake tin with butter and sprinkle with breadcrumbs. Place the mixture in the tin and bake in a moderate oven for about 20 minutes. Turn out on to a plate and serve. It will turn out in the form of a 'baba'.

Bacon balls
(Danish)

1 oz. butter
1 oz. flour
¼ pint milk
8 oz. cooked, minced bacon
1 teasp. chopped parsley
salt

pepper
nutmeg
½ teasp. mustard (already made)
1 beaten egg
dried breadcrumbs
fat for frying

Melt the butter in a saucepan, add the flour and stir for 1–2 minutes. Add the milk and cook until mixture thickens. Add the bacon, parsley, mustard, salt, pepper and nutmeg to taste. Allow mixture to cool, then form into balls. Dip the balls into the beaten egg, roll in breadcrumbs and fry in deep fat.

Cheese balls
(*Danish*)

4 oz. grated cheese (Gruyère or Cheddar)	½ teasp. mustard (already made)
	salt
¼ cup dried breadcrumbs	pepper
1 egg	fat for frying

Mix the breadcrumbs with the grated cheese and season with salt and pepper. Add the mustard and bind this mixture with the beaten egg. Shape into small balls and roll the balls in breadcrumbs. Fry in deep fat until golden brown. Drain and serve.

Cheese and bread pudding: Kase und Brotauflauf
(*German*)

12 oz. stale, white bread (sliced and buttered)	salt
	pepper
4 eggs	nutmeg
1 pint milk	2 tablesp. grated Parmesan cheese
8 oz. grated Gruyère cheese	

Arrange the sliced bread in layers in a greased fireproof dish. Beat the eggs and add the milk, grated Gruyère cheese, salt, pepper and nutmeg. Blend well and pour the mixture over the bread. Sprinkle with Parmesan cheese and leave to stand for 30 minutes. Pre-heat the oven to 350° F. or Gas reg. 4, and bake the pudding for about 45 minutes or until the top is golden in colour.

Cheese slices: Kaseküchlein
(*Austrian*)

8 oz. stale, sliced white bread	salt
8 oz. grated Gruyère or Cheddar cheese	pepper
	1½ cups of milk
2 eggs	butter for frying

Cut the crust off the bread slices and cut each slice diagonally across. Mix the grated cheese with an egg and 4 tablespoons of milk. Season with salt and pepper. Spread the cheese mixture on half of the bread slices. Cover with the other half. Press firmly and dip the slices first in milk and then in beaten egg. Fry on both sides in hot butter until golden brown in colour. Drain and serve.

Cheese croquettes: Luzerner Kasecroquetten
(*Swiss*)

4 oz. grated Gruyère cheese	salt
4 tablesp. flour	pepper
2 oz. butter	1 beaten egg
1 pint milk	flour and fat for frying
2 egg yolks	

Melt the butter and stir in the 4 tablespoons of flour. Gradually add the milk and bring to the boil. Cook for a few minutes, then add the grated cheese. Blend well and remove from the heat. The mixture should be thick. Add the egg yolks, season with salt and pepper and return to the heat, but do not allow to boil again. Stir until the eggs are well blended. Make sure the mixture remains thick. Grease a baking tin and spread the mixture on it to a thickness of 1 inch. Cool, and when cold, cut into long strips (about $2\frac{1}{2} \times 1$ inches), dip the strips in the beaten egg and coat with flour. Fry in hot deep fat until golden brown on both sides. Drain and serve.

Cheese on skewers
(*Swiss*)

8 oz. Gruyère or Cheddar cheese	salt
thick slices of bread, one day old	flour
1 beaten egg	fat for frying
milk	water

Cut the bread and cheese into small equal squares and spear them alternately on small skewers. Dip in milk, roll in flour, dip in the beaten egg mixed with a little water and salt. Roll in flour again and fry in hot fat, turning the skewers until the cheese and bread mixture is golden brown on all sides.

Place a small bowl containing tomato sauce in the centre of a round dish. Arrange the skewers round the bowl.

Chicken shami kebabs
(*Indian*)
This recipe is to be found in Section Six.

Cottage cheese fritters: Levaniot migvina
(*Israeli*)

1 tablesp. finely chopped onion	1 egg
2 tablesp. oil	salt
8 oz. cottage cheese	pepper
3 tablesp. fresh breadcrumbs	oil for frying
1 tablesp. chopped parsley	

Sauté the onion in oil but do not brown. Cool a little and mix with the cheese, breadcrumbs and parsley. Season with salt and pepper and bind with the egg. Form mixture into very small pancakes and fry in hot oil until golden in colour. Drain and serve.

Croûtons with onions: Grzanki z cebula
(*Polish*)

1 lb. sliced onions	juice of ½ lemon
water	2 oz. grated Parmesan cheese
1 oz. butter	salt
1 tablesp. flour	French bread for croûtons
½ cup stock	

Put the onions into a saucepan containing cold water. Bring to the boil and cook on a low heat for a few minutes. Drain onions. Heat the fat in frying-pan and sauté the onion slices, but do not brown them. Remove the onion and add the flour and, if needed, a little more butter. Stir in the flour and gradually add the stock and lemon juice. Return the onion to the pan, season with salt and stir in half of the grated cheese. Mix well and cook until the liquid has been absorbed and the mixture is well blended. Cut up bread to form croûtons and place them on a baking tray. Put some of the onion mixture on each croûton and sprinkle with the remaining cheese. Put a blob of butter on top. Bake in a hot oven (475° F., Gas reg. 7) for about 10 minutes or until the cheese on top is melted and the croûtons are well browned.

Eggs à la Suisse
(*Swiss*)

1 egg per person	pepper
grated cheese	cream
salt	

Cover the bottom of buttered ramekins with grated cheese. Slide an egg into each, sprinkle with salt and pepper and cover with teaspoon of cream. Top with a layer of grated cheese and bake in a moderate oven for 15 minutes.

Eggs akuri
(Parsee)

6 hard-boiled eggs	2 tomatoes, cut in small pieces
ghee or oil for frying	1 tablesp. chopped fresh coriander
1 large onion, chopped	leaves
4 green chillies, chopped	1 teasp. turmeric powder
1 teasp. lemon juice	salt
2 teasp. sugar	

Carefully remove the egg yolks from the whites. Slice the whites thinly. Heat the ghee or oil and fry the chopped onion lightly, then add the chillies, tomatoes and coriander. Cook for 5–7 minutes then add the turmeric and the sliced egg whites. Cook for a few minutes longer, then put in the egg yolks, sprinkle with lemon juice and sugar and serve hot.

Egg and aubergine: Hatzilim im Beytzim
(Israeli)

1 large or 2 small aubergines	2 hard-boiled eggs
1 medium onion, sliced	salt
3 tablesp. oil	pepper

Peel the aubergine, slice and sprinkle with salt. Leave to stand for about 30 minutes, then drain and dry on a paper towel.

Heat the oil in a frying-pan and sauté lightly the sliced onion. Remove from pan. In the same fat fry the aubergine slices until light brown and cooked through. Add more fat if necessary. Remove from pan. Chop finely, or pass through a mincer, the fried onion, aubergine and the shelled, boiled eggs. Season with salt and pepper to taste.

Note: This is usually known as 'mock liver pâté', and may also be served cold.

Eggs Imperial
(Austrian)

6 eggs	2 tablesp. Madeira
6 thick slices of white bread	butter
8 oz. sliced mushrooms	salt
½ pint white sauce	

Cook the mushrooms in butter and mix them with the Maderia and the sauce. Remove the crust from the bread slices and scoop out the inside leaving a ¼-inch shell. Spread the shell all over with soft butter and place on a greased tin. Fill the hollowed cases with the mushroom mixture. Make a dent in the mixture with the back of a spoon and break an egg into each. Season with salt and dot with butter. Bake in a moderate oven for about 10 minutes, or until the eggs are set.

Eggs Provençale
(French)

1 egg per person	pepper
1 large, ripe tomato per person	grated Parmesan cheese
garlic juice	fried parsley
salt	

Cut off the tops of the tomatoes and scoop out the pulp. Sprinkle the inside with salt, pepper and a few drops of garlic juice. Bake in a moderate oven for about 5 minutes. Remove from the oven. Drop an egg into each tomato, sprinkle the top with cheese, dot with butter and return to the oven for about another 10 minutes, or until the eggs are set. Garnish with fried parsley.

Stuffed eggs: Jajka faszerowane
(Polish)

6 hard-boiled eggs in their shells	salt
1 dessertsp. chopped chives or the green part of some spring onions	pepper
	dried breadcrumbs
	butter for frying
1 raw egg	fried parsley

With a sharp knife cut the unshelled eggs lengthwise. Scoop out the insides carefully so that you do not damage the shell. Chop the eggs finely and add the chives or onions. Season with salt and pepper and mix in the raw egg. Heat a little butter in a frying-pan and lightly fry the mixture. Remove from the heat and fill each shell with the mixture. Sprinkle with breadcrumbs and fry in hot butter with the stuffed part of the egg down. Serve garnished with fried parsley.
Note: The same stuffing could be served in ramekin dishes and baked for a few minutes in a hot oven.

Eggs surprise
(*Polish*)

1 egg per person
juice of ½ lemon
water
salt
1 or 2 raw beaten eggs

flour
grated Parmesan cheese
dried breadcrumbs
butter for frying

Poach the eggs in water to which the lemon juice has been added. When the eggs are set, remove them carefully from the pan and leave them to drain in a colander. When the eggs are dry, dip them carefully first in the flour (seasoned with salt), then in the beaten egg and finally sprinkle them with cheese. Coat the eggs with breadcrumbs and fry in hot butter until golden brown on both sides.

Green pea patties: Muttar ka samosa
(*Parsee*)

1 lb. potatoes
2 tablesp. cornflour
4 oz. green peas
ghee or oil for frying
2 tablesp. grated coconut
2 green chillies, chopped

2 tablesp. chopped fresh coriander
   leaves
½ teasp. turmeric powder
1 teasp. sugar
1 teasp. salt
½ teasp. chilli powder
semolina

Boil the potatoes, mash them and mix with the cornflour. Knead into a pliable paste. Boil the peas and mash or pound them coarsely. Fry the mashed peas in 2 tablespoons of ghee or oil, add the grated coconut, chillies, coriander, turmeric, sugar, salt and chilli powder. Stir for a few minutes and remove from the heat. Divide the potato paste into small pieces about the size of a walnut, flatten them on a floured board and place ½ teaspoon of the pea mixture on each. Close up the circles and shape them into small balls or flatten them again. Dust the patties with semolina and fry in hot oil or ghee till golden brown.

Ham rolls
(*Scandinavian*)

1 oz. butter
1 oz. flour
¼ pint milk
8 slices of cooked ham
6 oz. mild cheese

2 egg yolks
salt
black pepper
2 tablesp. tomato purée

Melt the butter in a saucepan and gradually mix in the flour. Cook for 1 minute, then slowly add a ¼ pint of milk. Cook for 3 minutes, stirring continuously. Remove white sauce from heat and cool. Stir in the egg yolks, salt and pepper. Cut up cheese into small cubes (leaving a few thin slices to garnish the top of the finished dish) and add these to the sauce. Put a dessertspoon of the sauce on each slice of ham, roll up the slice and place it in an ovenproof dish. Cover the rolled slices with the tomato purée which has been mixed with 4 tablespoons of milk. Pour the remainder of the cheese sauce on top. Cook in a pre-heated hot oven (425° F., Gas reg. 7) for about 15 minutes. Decorate with the remainder of the cheese and serve.

Ham rolls with cheese: Schinkerrollchen mit Kase
(Swiss)

4 oz. sliced ham
4 oz. mild, soft cheese

fat for frying
lettuce and tomatoes for garnish

Cut the ham into squares (about 3 × 3 inches) and cover each with a thin slice of cheese. Roll the ham and cheese and secure with a toothpick. Heat fat in a frying-pan and fry the rolls. Serve on a bed of lettuce leaves, and garnish with slices of tomato.

Kofta curry
(Pakistani)

This recipe is given in Section Six.

Masala Dosai
(Indian)

For the pancake
8 oz. semolina
1½ cups water
1 teasp. curd or yoghurt
ghee or oil for frying

For the filling
4 medium-sized potatoes
1 large onion, sliced
2 green chillies
½ inch fresh ginger, chopped
½ teasp. mustard seeds
½ teasp. turmeric powder
salt

To prepare pancake: Put the semolina in a bowl, add water, curd or yoghurt, and salt and beat well until a creamy batter is formed. Leave overnight. The next day, when ready to use it, heat some oil or ghee in a frying-pan and pour 2 tablespoons of the semolina mixture into it, spreading it over the pan evenly as you would for an ordinary pancake. Cover with a lid and cook for a minute or two. Remove the lid and place a little of the filling on one side of the pancake then fold the other over. Add a little more fat and fry the 'dosai' turning it until crisp. *To prepare the filling:* Boil the potatoes and when cooked, skin and mash them. Heat a little ghee or oil in a frying-pan and fry the mustard seeds until they begin to crackle. Add the sliced onion, chillies, ginger and turmeric. Cook until the onion is lightly browned. Add the mashed potato. Blend well and fry for 5 minutes.

Onion tart
(*French*)

For the case
6 oz. flour
4 oz. butter
water
salt

For the filling
1 lb. onions, chopped
2 oz. butter
1 breakfast cup cream or top of milk
2 eggs
salt
pepper
pinch nutmeg
3 tablesp. grated cheese

To prepare the case: Rub the butter into the flour, seasoned with salt, and add a little cold water to make a firm dough. Roll it out thinly and line a 7–8-inch greased flan case.
To prepare filling: Melt the butter in a pan and sauté the chopped onion till soft but not brown. Beat the eggs and mix with the cream or milk and add the seasoning. Add the onions to this mixture and stir in the grated cheese. Pour the mixture into the case and bake in a pre-heated oven (375° F., Gas reg. 5) for about 40–45 minutes. Serve cut into wedges.
Note: This can also be served cold.

Potato bliny
(*Estonian*)

1 bread roll (about 2 oz.)
1 large potato, grated
2 teasp. sour cream
milk

salt
1 egg
⅓ oz. yeast
fat for frying

c

Remove the crust from the bread roll and cut it into pieces. Place in a bowl and pour about ½ cup of milk over it. Leave this to soak. When the roll is well saturated, either mash it with a fork or pass it through a sieve. Then mix it with the grated potato. (There should be about ½ cupful of pulp). Add the sour cream, salt and the egg yolk. Dissolve the yeast in a tablespoon of lukewarm milk and stir into the potato mixture. Fold in the stiffly-beaten egg white. Mix well, cover with a cloth and leave in a warm place for about 2 hours to rise. (The batter should have the consistency of thick cream. If when you come to use it you find it too thin, carefully sprinkle in a tablespoon of flour; if it is too thick, add a little milk.) Heat the fat in a frying-pan until smoking, then pour 1 tablespoon of the batter into the fat. Spread thinly and fry quickly on both sides. Remove to a hot dish. Keep the blinis hot until all the batter has been used.

Salmon patties: Barquettes au saumon
(French)

8 oz. puff pastry	½ cup white sauce
8 oz. cooked or tinned salmon	½ teasp. anchovy essence

Roll out the pastry and line boat-shaped baking cases with it. Flake the fish and add this and the anchovy essence to the white sauce. Mix well and three-quarters fill the baking cases with this mixture. Cover with a thin layer of pastry. Brush with beaten egg and bake in a pre-heated oven (425° F., Gas reg. 7) for 15 minutes.

Semolina patties
(Indian)

4 oz. semolina	1 teasp. turmeric powder
¾–1 pint water	1 egg
salt	flour
1 tablesp. coriander leaves, chopped	ghee or oil for frying

Heat 2 tablespoons of ghee or oil in a pan, add the semolina and fry lightly. Add the water and salt and cook until the mixture is thick, stirring continuously. When the mixture is nearly cooked add the coriander and turmeric. Cool on a greased plate. When cold, cut into small patties. Dip them in beaten egg, then in flour and fry in hot oil until golden in colour. Drain and serve.

Asparagus soup: Crême d'asperges
(*French*)

2½ oz. butter
1 oz. cornflour
3 pints stock or water
1 lb. asparagus tips

2 egg yolks
2 tablesp. thick cream
salt

Heat the stock or water. Melt 2 oz. butter and stir in the cornflour. Cook for a minute and then add the hot liquid, stirring continuously. Add most of the asparagus tips. Simmer for 1 hour. Mash the asparagus tips and pass everything through a sieve. Beat the egg yolks with the cream and add to the liquid. Add the rest of the butter in very small pieces, add salt to taste and garnish the soup with the rest of the asparagus tips.

Note: If tinned asparagus is used for this soup, the cooking time should be reduced to 30 minutes.

Barley soup: Krupnik
(*Polish*)

soup bones
1 carrot
½ stalk celery
½ onion or 1 leek
¼ oz. dried mushrooms (soaked in water)

3 oz. fine barley
1½ oz. butter
1½ pint water
2 raw potatoes
1 tablesp. chopped dill or parsley
salt

Boil the soup bones with carrot, onion or leek, celery, mushrooms and the water in which the mushrooms have been soaked. Drain and retain the carrot, celery and mushrooms. The stock should measure 1½ pints.

In a separate saucepan simmer the washed barley in 1½ pints of water with the addition of 1½ oz. butter. When the barley is soft and glutinous add to it the stock and stir well. Cut the potatoes into cubes and add to the soup together with the boiled and sliced carrot, celery and mushrooms. Season with salt and continue cooking until the potatoes are done. Before serving add the dill or parsley.

Note: The same soup can be made with vegetable stock, only with 2–3 tablespoons of cream added towards the end of cooking.

Beer soup: Øl suppe
(*Danish*)

2 pints beer	3 egg yolks
2 cloves	½ cup cream
1 small stick cinnamon	bread croûtons
3 oz. sugar	

Bring the beer to the boil with the cloves, cinnamon and sugar. Beat the egg yolks until light and frothy and slowly add a little of the hot beer. Add the cream and pour the mixture into the hot beer. Do not boil after the cream and yolks have been added. Remove the cinnamon and cloves and serve the soup with croûtons made with French bread.

Beetroot with yoghurt soup: Chlodnik
(*Polish*)

1 lb. young beetroots	½ cup sour cream
1 cucumber	1 tablesp. chopped fresh dill
salt	juice of 2 lemons
sugar	2 hard-boiled eggs
2 cups yoghurt	

Wash and cut the beetroot including some of the leaves. Cook it in very little water to which a pinch of salt and sugar have been added. Peel the cucumber and cut into small cubes. When the beetroot is tender, strain and keep the liquid and a few leaves and leave to cool. Whip the yoghurt with the cream, add the lemon juice and pour into the cold beetroot liquid. Cut the hard-boiled eggs into wedges and add these and a few of the beetroot leaves to the liquid. Mix well and leave to chill.

Borstch
(*Ukranian*)

1 lb. pork with bones	2 beetroots, cut into strips
3 dried mushrooms, soaked in water	8 oz. cabbage, shredded
2 small onions	3 oz. small haricot beans (soaked overnight and cooked)
small piece of celery	juice of lemon to taste
salt	½ cup sour cream
1 carrot, cut into strips	3 pints water
1 lb. tomatoes, cooked and passed through sieve	1 oz. butter or lard

Place the meat in a saucepan with the water. Bring to the boil and skim. Add the mushrooms together with the water in which they were soaked, 1 onion, garlic and celery. Season with salt and simmer on a low heat for 1½–2 hours. Strain. Reserve stock and cut the meat into cubes. Chop the other onion and sauté it, with the carrot, in the heated butter or lard, in a separate saucepan. Add the tomato pulp, beetroot and cabbage and continue cooking on a slow heat until the vegetables are tender, then add the stock and more salt if needed. Bring to the boil, add haricot beans, meat cubes and lemon juice to taste. Stir in sour cream and serve.

Note: Hard-boiled eggs can be added. If they are, they should be cut into wedges and placed in the dish in which the soup is served.

Calf's brain soup
(Swiss)

1 calf's brain	2 tablesp. flour
2 oz. butter	2½ pints stock
1 small sliced onion	2 egg yolks
salt	chopped parsley

Wash the brain well. Remove the skin. Heat the butter in a saucepan and sauté the onion until it is golden in colour. Add the brain, sprinkle with flour and fry for a few minutes. Add enough stock to mix the flour to a smooth paste and continue cooking for 10 minutes. Add the rest of the stock. Bring to the boil. Season with salt and remove from the heat. Beat the egg yolks and add them. Sprinkle with chopped parsley and serve.

Cold soup: Doogh Khiar
(Persian)

2 cups yoghurt	1 teasp. fresh basil, chopped
1 chopped cucumber	some chopped walnuts
1 chopped spring onion	2 oz. sultanas
1 teasp. chopped mint	salt

Beat the yoghurt and mix with the chopped cucumber, onions, mint and basil. Stir in the walnuts and sultanas and season with salt. Serve very cold.

Cold soup: Gazpacho
(*Spanish*)

2 large tomatoes	salt
1 green pepper	pepper
1 onion	2 cups tomato juice
1 clove garlic	1 diced cucumber
2 tablesp. olive oil	2 slices of white bread cut into
2 tablesp. wine vinegar or 3	small cubes
tablesp. lemon juice	

Chop finely the tomatoes, pepper, onion and garlic. Place all into a bowl, add the olive oil, vinegar or lemon juice and mix well. Season with salt and pepper and stir in the tomato juice. Chill for several hours. Before serving add the diced cucumber and bread cubes.

Cream of celery soup: Crema di sedani
(*Italian*)

1½ lb. celery	salt
2 carrots	pepper
1 leek	2 beaten egg yolks
2 oz. butter	½ cup cream
2½ pints water	2 tablesp. grated Parmesan cheese

After scraping the celery, peeling the carrots and washing the leek, slice all the vegetables and sauté them in butter in a saucepan for several minutes. Add about a cup of hot water and continue cooking on a slow heat until the vegetables are soft, then pass them through a strainer or blend them in a liquidizer. Return the purée to the saucepan, add the rest of the water, salt, and pepper. Bring to the boil and simmer for a few minutes. Remove from the heat. Beat the egg yolks with the cream and add the grated cheese. Blend a little of the hot soup into this mixture. Add mixture to the soup, stirring well all the time. Do not boil or the eggs will curdle.

Egg soup: Sopa de Yemas
(*Spanish*)

3 pints stock	3 tablesp. chopped, cooked
4 egg yolks	chicken
1 lemon (juice)	bread croûtons
	salt, pepper

of each toast with grated cheese. Place a piece of toast in each individual soup bowl or half fill ovenproof soup tureen with toast slices and pour the hot soup over them. Sprinkle the top with more grated cheese and set the tureen or bowls under a hot grill or in a hot oven until the cheese is sizzling.

Potato soup: Kartoffelsuppe
(German)

1 lb. potatoes	salt
2 leeks	1½ oz. butter
2 pints water	½ cup thick cream

Peel the potatoes and cut them into pieces. Clean and slice the leeks. Put the potatoes and leeks into a saucepan and cover them with the water. Bring to the boil and simmer gently until the vegetables are cooked. Pass everything through a sieve and return the pulp and the liquid to the pan. Season with salt, add the butter and simmer for a few minutes. Stir in the cream, bring to the boil and serve.

Sauerkraut soup: Schi
(Russian)

½ lb. pork	3–4 dried mushrooms, soaked in
2 small onions	water
1 carrot	1 oz. lard
½ stalk celery	1 tablesp. flour
salt	4 oz. continental sausage (optional)
1 lb. sauerkraut	
water	

Put the meat in a saucepan and cover it with water. Bring to the boil. Skim and add 1 onion and the carrot and celery. Season with salt and simmer until the meat is tender. Strain, and keep the stock and meat.

In a separate saucepan, boil the sauerkraut in 1 pint of water. When it is tender add the meat stock and the meat cut into small pieces. Cut the mushrooms into strips and add them.

Melt the lard in a frying-pan. Chop the other onion, sauté it until soft and transparent, then add the flour and a little of the soup to make a roux. Add the roux to the soup, bring to the boil and cook for 30 minutes. Season with salt as required and (if using) add the sausage cut into small pieces.

Note: Boiled potatoes may be served with the soup.

Spinach soup: Spenatova Polevka
(*Czechoslovakian*)

For the soup:
1½ lb. spinach
1 oz. butter
1 tablesp. flour
½ cup thick cream
salt
2 pints water

For the croûtons:
2 oz. bread rolls or a French roll
2 slices cooked ham
flour
milk
1 egg
butter or lard for frying

To make the soup: Wash the spinach several times. Place in a deep saucepan and cover with the water. Cook for about 10 minutes and drain. Keep the water. Chop up the spinach finely. Heat the butter in a saucepan and add the flour to make a roux, then gradually add some of the spinach water. When this is well blended add the rest of the water and the spinach. If there is not enough spinach water, add more water or milk. Season with salt and stir in cream. Bring to the boil and serve with croûtons.

To make the croûtons: Slice the rolls, remove the crust and cut into rounds with a pastry cutter. Moisten the rounds with milk. Place a slice of ham between two rounds, dip it in egg, roll it in flour and fry on both sides till golden brown. Serve on a separate dish.

Thai noodle soup
(*Siamese*)

1 medium-sized chicken
1 teasp. salt
¼ teasp. ve-tsin (monosodium glutamate)
¼ teasp. black pepper

3 pints water
8 oz. noodles
6 oz. bean sprouts or 1 small tin
3 spring onions
salt

Skin the chicken and remove the bones. Put the skin and bones in a saucepan, add water and bring to the boil. Skim, season with salt and simmer on a low heat for 1 hour. Strain and keep the stock.

Mince the chicken finely, add a little salt and pepper and the ve-tsin. Mix well and form into small balls. Bring the chicken stock to the boil, drop in the chicken balls, and simmer gently for 10 minutes. Add the noodles and cook until they are done. Add the bean sprouts (drained if tinned), sliced spring onions including some of the green part, season to taste and cook for only 2 minutes.

Vegetable broth: Kawlata
(*Maltese*)

12 oz. pork meat (any cheap cut)	2 big potatoes, cubed
1 large onion, chopped	2 tablesp. tomato purée
2 carrots, cut into cubes	salt
2 stalks celery, sliced	pepper
½ small cauliflower, cut into pieces	2 tablesp. fine barley
½ small marrow, cut into cubes	grated cheese

Place the meat in a large pan, cover with water and bring to the boil. Skim and continue cooking until the meat is half done. Add the chopped onion, carrots, celery, cauliflower and the marrow and cook for a few minutes, then add the cubed potatoes, the tomato purée and the barley. Season with salt and pepper. Cover the pan and simmer on a low heat until the meat is tender and all vegetables cooked. Add hot water during the cooking to bring the soup to the desired consistency.

Serve the soup with grated cheese.

The meat can be served separately or cut into cubes and mixed with the soup.

Vichyssoise
(*French*)

1 sliced medium-sized onion	1 cup milk
3 or 4 sliced leeks (white part only)	1 cup cream
1 oz. butter or margarine	salt
1 lb. potatoes	pepper
4 cups chicken stock	chopped chives

Heat the butter in a saucepan, add the onion and leeks and sauté until soft and transparent. Peel and slice the potatoes and add these. Pour the stock into the pan, bring it to the boil, cover the saucepan and simmer for about 40 minutes or until the potatoes are done. Strain and rub potatoes and vegetables through a sieve, or blend everything in a liquidizer. Put everything back into the saucepan, add the milk and bring it to the boil. Remove from the heat, season with salt and pepper and allow to cool. When cold add the cream and chill. Serve very cold and sprinkled with chopped chives.

D

Heat the oil or lard in a heavy frying-pan and fry the onion until it turns golden in colour. Add the green pepper and continue cooking on a low heat. When the pepper is soft, add the chopped tomatoes and seasoning. Cover the pan and cook mixture until it thickens. Beat the eggs and pour them into the mixture. Stir gently as for ordinary scrambled eggs.

Eggs with potatoes: Uova con patate
(*Italian*)

1 lb. potatoes	2 oz. Mozzarella or Bel Paese
½ oz. butter	cheese
3 tablesp. milk	4 eggs
salt	grated Parmesan cheese
pepper	

Boil the potatoes in their skins. Peel them and beat in butter and milk to make a creamy purée. Season with salt and pepper. Grease a shallow ovenproof dish and put slices of Mozzarella or Bel Paese cheese on the bottom. Cover with potato purée. Make four holes in the purée with the back of a spoon and break an egg into each hollow. Sprinkle with grated Parmesan cheese, dot with butter and bake in a moderate oven until the eggs are set and the cheese melted.

Scrambled eggs: Akuri
(*Parsee*)

4 eggs	salt
1 large onion, chopped	pinch red chilli powder
2 cloves garlic, finely chopped	1½ oz. butter for frying
3 medium-sized tomatoes, chopped	

Break eggs into a bowl and beat lightly. Heat the butter in a frying-pan and sauté onion and garlic but do not brown. Add chopped tomatoes and continue frying until they are reduced to a pulp. Add the beaten egg and stir briskly. Season with salt and chilli powder.

Scrambled eggs Santelli
(*Hungarian*)

4 rashers streaky bacon	4 eggs
2 oz. sliced garlic sausage	salt
1 medium-sized green pepper	grated Parmesan cheese
2 medium-sized tomatoes	

Cut the bacon rashers into small pieces and fry until crisp. Remove from the pan. Into the fat in the pan add the sausage and sliced green pepper. Cook slowly for a minute or two and add the peeled and sliced tomatoes. Season with salt and cook until the tomatoes are ready. Beat the eggs lightly and mix in the bacon pieces. Pour over the vegetable mixture. Cook, stirring all the time, and when ready sprinkle with grated Parmesan cheese.

Stuffed eggs
(*Indian*)

For the stuffed eggs:	For the tomato sauce:
4 hard-boiled eggs	1 small onion, finely sliced
1 dessertsp. melted ghee or butter	½ lb. ripe tomatoes, sliced
1 thick slice bread (with crust removed)	1 dessertsp. fresh coriander leaves, chopped
1 green chilli, finely chopped	1 tablesp. ghee or oil
1 teasp. finely chopped onion	½ teasp. of garam masala
salt	½ teasp. chilli powder
water	salt
	water

To prepare the eggs: Shell the hard-boiled eggs and cut them into halves lengthways. Remove the yolks and place them in a bowl. Soak the bread in water, squeeze dry and mash well. Add the bread to the egg yolks and mix together to a smooth paste. Add the melted ghee or butter, onion, chilli and salt and mix well. Fill the egg whites with the stuffing. Place the eggs in an ovenproof dish and pour the prepared tomato sauce over them. Cover the dish and put into a pre-heated oven. Cook at a moderate heat for about 30 minutes. Serve with hot chupattis, *see* Section Seven.

To prepare the tomato sauce: Heat the ghee or oil in a frying-pan. Sauté the onion till soft but not brown. Add all the other ingredients and cook till well blended, adding a little water if necessary. A fairly thick sauce should be formed.

OMELETTES

Aubergine omelette: Cookoo badenjan
(*Persian*)

2 small aubergines or 1 big one, sliced
4 eggs
salt
pepper
4 oz. butter or cooking fat for frying

Peel and slice the aubergine, sprinkle with salt and leave for 30 minutes. Drain and dry on a kitchen towel. Heat the fat in a frying-pan and fry the slices until tender. Remove from fat and chop finely. Break the eggs into a bowl, beat them lightly and add the chopped aubergines, salt and pepper. Add more fat to the frying-pan and heat, then pour in the egg mixture. Fry on a low heat or bake in a slow oven until omelette is set and golden brown in colour. Slide omelette on to a hot dish.

Omelette
(*Parsee*)

3 eggs
1 medium-sized onion
1 tablesp. coriander leaves
2 green chillies
1 clove garlic
½ inch fresh ginger
2 teasp. tomato or mango chutney
1 teasp. water
salt
ghee or oil for frying

Break the eggs into a bowl and beat slightly. Grind the onion, coriander leaves, chillies, garlic and ginger and mix with the beaten eggs. Add the chutney and water and mix well. Heat ghee or oil in a frying-pan and pour in mixture. Fry the omelette on one side. Turn and cook the other side. Do not fold over. Slide omelette on to a hot dish.

Omelette with caviar: Omlet s ikroy
(*Russian*)

4 eggs
1 tablesp. single cream
black caviar
salt
butter for frying

Heat the butter in an omelette pan. Break the eggs into a bowl, beat them and mix in salt and cream. Just before the butter in the pan turns brown pour in half the egg mixture. Shake the pan so that the mixture spreads evenly over it. Keep on shaking and tilting the pan as the mixture cooks, loosening the edges so that the uncooked part can run on to the pan. When the mixture is set, slide the omelette on to a hot dish. Repeat for second omelette. Decorate the top with strips or a lattice pattern made from caviar.

Omelette with fried bread: Omelette de croûton
(*French*)

1 slice bread with crust removed	salt
butter for frying	pepper
2 eggs	nutmeg (optional)
2 teasp. grated cheese	

Cut the bread into small squares and fry in hot butter until golden brown and crisp. Remove from the frying-pan. Break the eggs into a bowl and beat them. Season with salt and pepper and add a pinch of nutmeg if liked. Re-heat the frying-pan and add more butter. Pour the beaten eggs into the hot fat and add the grated cheese. Cook as above. When the omelette is set, add the fried croûtons, fold over quickly and slide on to a hot dish.

Spice omelette
(*Indian*)

3 eggs	pepper
2 tablesp. besan flour (gram flour)	½ teasp. coriander powder
	½ teasp. cardamom powder
1 medium-sized onion sliced	4 tablesp. curd (sour milk)
salt	3 tablesp. ghee or oil for frying

Break the eggs into a bowl and gradually add the flour, sliced onion, salt and pepper, stirring all the time. Combine the coriander powder and cardamon powder with the curd in a separate bowl, and add this to the egg mixture. Beat until smooth. Heat the ghee or oil in a frying-pan and add the mixture. Cook until set. Do not fold over. Slide omelette on to a hot dish and serve.

SECTION FOUR

Fish Dishes

Balaton carp (*Hungarian*)
Baked whiting (*French*)
Bengali fish curry (*Indian*)
Carp in jelly (*Jewish*)
Fish cutlets (*Czechoslovakian*)
Fish in marinade (*Yugoslav*)
Fish pie (*Russian*)
Fish with cream (*German*)
Fish with horseradish (*Polish*)
Fish with mushrooms (*Polish*)
Fish with tomatoes (*Dalmation*)
Fish with vegetables
 (*Portuguese*)
Greek fish (*Greek*)

King prawns (*Parsee*)
Lobster thermidor (*French*)
Malayan fried fish (*Malaysian*)
Perch in batter (*French*)
Prawn and egg curry (*Indian*)
Prawns and green peas (*Chinese*)
Sambal goreng Java (*Indonesian*)
Scandinavian herrings
 (*Scandinavian*)
Sole à la meunière (*French*)
Sweet and sour fish (*Chinese*)
Trout in wine (*Swiss*)
Fish with onions (*Turkish*)

Balaton carp
(*Hungarian*)

2 lb. carp	3 tomatoes, sliced
4 oz. bacon	2 green peppers, sliced
salt	½ cup sour cream
paprika	1 teasp. flour
3 large potatoes	2 oz. butter
1 onion, sliced	

Scale and wash the fish. Rub well with salt and paprika and make small incisions across the fish. Leave the head and tail on. Place thin slices of bacon in the incisions. Peel the potatoes and parboil them. Cut into slices. Grease an ovenproof dish and cover the bottom with the potato slices. Place the fish on the potatoes and cover with sliced onion, tomatoes and green peppers. Pour melted butter over the fish and vegetables and put in a pre-heated oven. Bake at 400° F., Gas reg. 6 for about 1 hour. When fish is half-cooked, add the cream blended with flour and continue cooking until completely cooked.

Baked whiting: Merlans au four
(*French*)

6 large whitings	1 glass dry white wine
salt	3 tablesp. thick cream
pepper	flour
butter	

Clean and gut the fish. Dry on a kitchen towel and sprinkle with salt. Roll lightly in flour and place in a buttered ovenproof dish. Dot with more butter and bake in a moderate oven for about 15 minutes. Take out dish from the oven and pour the wine over the fish, then spread the cream over it. Season with salt and pepper and return to the oven for about another 7 minutes.

Bengali fish curry
(*Indian*)

1 lb. white fish	2 bay leaves
4 red chillies	1 large sliced onion
1 inch fresh ginger	1 teasp. garam masala
1 teasp. turmeric powder	4 tablesp. ghee or oil
2 teasp. salt	2 tablesp. mustard oil
4 green chillies	a few chopped coriander leaves
1 cup curd	

Clean and gut the fish and cut it into 2-inch squares. Grind the red chillies with the ginger and turmeric and rub this mixture into the fish pieces. Season with salt. Cut the green chillies lengthways and mix with the curd. Add this to the fish and leave for about 30 minutes.

Heat the ghee or oil with the mustard oil in a pan and sauté the sliced onion lightly. Add the bay leaves and garam masala and fry until slightly brown, then add the fish pieces. Cover the pan and simmer on a low heat for about 15 minutes or until fish is cooked and the gravy rich and thick. Shake the pan occasionally to prevent the fish sticking to the pan. Garnish with chopped coriander leaves and serve with boiled rice (*see* Section Seven).

Carp in jelly
(*Jewish*)

2 lb. carp	salt
2 large sliced onions	pepper
2–3 sliced carrots	1 teasp. sugar
1 oz. butter	

Scale and clean the fish and cut into slices. Season with salt and pepper. Put the onions and carrots into a large saucepan and dot with butter. Place the slices of fish on top of the vegetables and sprinkle with sugar. Cover with water and simmer gently for 1–1½ hours, or until the stock is reduced by half and the fish tender. Leave the fish to cool in the liquid, then take it out carefully and place on a serving dish. Pass the vegetables through a sieve, then return to the liquid in the pan. Mix all together and pour over the fish. Leave to set in a cool place.

Fish cutlets: Z ryby kotlety
(*Czechoslovakian*)

1 lb. cod	salt
1 small bread roll soaked in milk	pepper
1 tablesp. chopped onion	dried breadcrumbs
½ oz. butter	oil or butter for frying
2 egg yolks	

Mince the fish and mix in a bowl with the bread roll, which has been squeezed dry. Heat some butter in a frying-pan, fry the chopped onion and add to the minced fish. Stir in the egg yolks and season with salt and pepper. Mix well. Dip your hands in water to make it easier to form the mixture into cutlets. Coat the cutlets in breadcrumbs. Heat some more oil or butter in a frying-pan and put cutlets in. Fry on both sides until golden brown. Serve with a caper or hollandaise sauce.

Fish in marinade: Marinada od ribe
(*Yugoslav*)

2 lb. mackerel or herrings	2 large onions, finely sliced
½ cup oil	salt
1 cup vinegar	pepper
1 cup water	2 sprigs fresh rosemary

Clean and bone the fish. Remove the skin and cut into fillets. Sprinkle with salt and pepper and dust with flour. Heat the oil in a frying-pan and fry the fish on both sides until it is cooked. Remove from the pan and cool. Mix the vinegar with the water and add to the oil in the pan. Add rosemary and a little pepper. Place layers of fish in a jar alternating with layers of thinly sliced onion. Pour the vinegar and oil mixture over the fish to cover. Seal the jar and leave in a cool place for two days before serving.

Fish pie: Kulebjak
(*Russian*)

8 oz. plain flour	3 oz. butter
½ oz. yeast	1 small onion, chopped
½ teasp. sugar	3 oz. rice
2 egg yolks	1 oz. dried mushrooms (optional)
⅛ pint milk	2 hard-boiled eggs
pinch salt	salt
4 oz. butter	pepper
1 lb. cod or halibut	

Sieve flour and salt into a bowl and make a hollow in the centre. Cream the yeast and sugar and add 2 tablespoons lukewarm milk. Pour this into the flour. Sprinkle a little of the flour on top of the yeast and leave in a warm place to rise. Add the rest of the milk and the egg yolks and knead into a soft dough. Cover and again leave in a warm place to rise. When the dough has doubled in bulk place it on a floured board and roll out into a square. Place the butter, cut into thin slices, on it and fold over like an envelope. Roll out again. Leave for 15 minutes. Repeat this process four times.

Boil the fish in very little water and 1½ oz. butter. When cooked, take out the bones. Boil the rice and drain. Heat the rest of the butter in a pan and fry the onion but do not brown it. (If mushrooms are used, soak them in water, drain and fry them in the butter after the onions.)

Roll out dough into an oblong about ½-inch thick. Put a layer of the cooked rice on the dough, sprinkle with onions and mushrooms and cover with the cooked, flaked fish. Sprinkle with melted butter and season with salt and pepper. Cut the hard-boiled eggs or chop them roughly and put them on top of the fish. Roll up dough like a Swiss roll and secure the edges. Place on a greased baking sheet, brush with beaten egg and leave to rise for 15–20 minutes. Pre-heat the oven at 400° F., Gas reg. 6 and bake for 35–40 minutes. Cut into slices and serve hot.

Fish with cream: Fisch mit Sahne
(German)

2 lb. white fish	*For the sauce:*
1 large sliced onion	2 oz. butter
1 bay leaf (optional)	¾ cup sour cream
salt	1 tablesp. flour
pepper	
water	

Heat butter in a large saucepan and lightly sauté the onion. Add the bay leaf (if liked). Clean, bone and skin the fish and cut into convenient slices. Add these to the saucepan. Season with salt and pepper and cover with water. Simmer gently in the covered saucepan until the fish is cooked. Take out the fish and put it on a warm serving dish.

To make the sauce: In a bowl blend flour and cream and add a little of the hot fish stock. Put this in a saucepan with enough fish stock to enable the finished sauce to cover the fish. Bring to the boil and simmer gently for a few minutes. Pour over fish.

Fish with horseradish: Ryba z Chrzanem
(*Polish*)

Pike or carp are most suitable for this dish, but it is also nice made from cod, halibut or haddock.

2 lb. fish, cleaned and scaled	1 oz. butter
1 onion, sliced	1 oz. flour
1 carrot, sliced	½ cup fish stock
1 small stalk celery, sliced	½ cup single cream
1 bay leaf	2–3 tablesp. horseradish
a few peppercorns	½ teasp. sugar
salt	lemon juice to taste
	salt
	water

Place the vegetables, peppercorns and bay leaf in a pan, cover with water, season with salt and simmer on a low heat until vegetables are tender. Strain the vegetable stock into a large pan and place the fish in it. (The fish can be cooked whole or sliced.) There should be enough vegetable stock to cover the fish and the stock should be hot, but not boiling. Simmer gently for about 30 minutes or until the fish is done. Remove carefully on to a hot serving dish and keep warm while preparing the sauce.

Make a roux with butter and flour and blend in the fish stock and the cream. Season to taste, add the horseradish, sugar and the lemon juice. Pour the sauce over the fish and serve.

Note: Instead of poaching the fish it can be baked. Liberally grease aluminium foil or greaseproof paper and place the fish on it. Sprinkle with salt and pepper and a little lemon juice. Wrap like a parcel and bake in a moderate oven (350° F., Gas reg. 5) for about 40 minutes.

Fish with mushrooms: Ryba z pieczarkami
(*Polish*)

2 lb. white fish	pepper
2½ oz. butter	1 cup sour cream
8 oz. sliced mushrooms	1 teasp. flour
1 small chopped onion	2 tablesp. water
salt	

E

Clean, bone and skin fish and place it in a greased ovenproof dish.
Melt 1½ oz. butter and pour it over the fish. Season with salt and bake
in a moderate oven for 10–15 minutes.

Heat rest of butter in a frying-pan and add the onion and mushrooms. Sauté these, add salt, pepper and water and simmer for 10
minutes with the lid on. Spread the mixture over the fish and pour the
cream blended with the flour over it. Return the fish to the oven and
cook for 15 minutes, or until the fish is done.

Fish with tomatoes: Brodetto
(Dalmatian)

2 lb. cod or habilut steaks	1 clove garlic, chopped
salt	2 lb. fresh tomatoes or 16-oz.
pepper	can tomatoes
flour for coating	oil for frying
1 medium-sized onion, chopped	

Clean the fish steaks and dust with flour. Heat the oil in a frying-pan.
Put in the fish steaks and fry lightly. Remove from the pan. In the
same oil fry the onion until light brown, add garlic and stir it quickly
to prevent burning. Add the tomatoes, which should have been peeled
and quartered if fresh, and cook for about 10 minutes. Add the fish,
season with salt and pepper, lower the heat and simmer very slowly
for about 30 minutes. The sauce should be thick and rich. Serve with
boiled rice (*see* Section Seven) or polenta.

Fish with vegetables: Peixe e legumes
(Portuguese)

2 lb. white fish (cod or halibut)	1 bay leaf
1 carrot	1 tablesp. oil
1 stalk celery	salt
1 onion, sliced	pepper
1 lb. tomatoes, sliced	water

Wash, clean and fillet the fish. Grease a fireproof dish and place the
fish in it. Season with salt.

Place all the vegetables and bay leaf in a pan with 4–5 tablespoons
water and 1 tablespoon oil. Cover and simmer until vegetables are
tender. Pass the cooked vegetables through a sieve and season with
salt and pepper. The sauce should be thick. Pour the sauce over the
fish, sprinkle with breadcrumbs, dot with butter and bake for about
30 minutes at 375° F., Gas reg. 5.

Greek fish: Psari Plaki
(Greek)

2 lb. cod or halibut	1 lb. tomatoes or
6 tablesp. oil	3–4 tablesp. tomato purée
2 large chopped onions	1 stalk celery, cut into thin pieces
salt	1 teasp. chopped fresh dill
pepper	½ cup water
½ teasp. sugar	lemon juice to taste

Clean the fish and cut it into portions. Heat the oil in a saucepan. Add the onions and sauté lightly. Add tomatoes or tomato purée, celery, salt and pepper, water and dill. Cover the pan and cook for about 15 minutes, or until the sauce has thickened. Dry the fish slices and put them into the sauce. Add the lemon juice and cook the fish on a low heat until it is tender and the sauce rich and thick. Remove the fish to a serving dish and cover with the sauce. Serve either hot or cold.

King prawns: Sondhia
(Parsee)

1 lb. king prawns	2 teasp. salt
3 cloves garlic	juice of ½ lemon
6 green chillies	¼ cup oil for frying
1 teasp. turmeric powder or	1 tablesp. chopped coriander
small piece turmeric	leaves
½ teasp. cumin seeds	

Clean and wash the prawns and remove the black veins. Grind the garlic, chillies, turmeric and cumin seeds and mix to a paste. Add salt and rub the prawns with the paste. Heat the oil in a pan and fry the prawns on a low heat till almost dry. Add 1 cup of water and cook till they are tender. Add lemon juice and chopped coriander leaves. Remove from pan to dish and serve.

Lobster thermidor: Homard thermidor
(French)

1 boiled lobster	pepper
1 oz. butter	dash paprika
1 oz. flour	1 tablesp. chopped parsley
½ cup milk	2 tablesp. sherry
½ cup thick cream	2 tablesp. grated Parmesan cheese
salt	

Cut the lobster into halves, remove meat and break it into small
pieces. In a pan, heat the butter, blend in the flour and stir in the milk.
Add the cream and cook until sauce has thickened, stirring constantly.
Season with salt and pepper and add the parsley, paprika and lobster
meat. Simmer for a few minutes longer and add the sherry. Fill the
lobster shells with this mixture and sprinkle with cheese. Bake in a very
hot oven 450° F., Gas reg. 8 for 5 minutes.

Malayan fried fish
(*Malaysian*)

1 lb. white fish	2 red chillies
1 teasp. turmeric powder or	salt
1 small piece turmeric	ghee or oil for frying

Grind salt, turmeric and chillies together. Clean, bone and skin the
fish and rub the salt, turmeric and chilli paste into it. Heat the oil in a
frying-pan and fry the fish on both sides till it is cooked.

Perch in batter: Perche à la Orly
(*French*)

Perch is a fresh-water fish with delicate and easily digestible flesh, but
if unobtainable use halibut or haddock.

2 lb. fish	*For batter:*
oil, or oil and butter mixed, for	1 egg
frying	½ cup milk
	salt
	1 teasp. melted butter or oil
	4 oz. flour
	½ teasp. baking powder

Scale and clean the fish and cut it into pieces about 3 inches wide.
Season with salt.

Beat the egg yolk with milk, add a pinch of salt and stir in the
melted butter or oil. Gradually add the sifted flour and the baking
powder. (The baking powder will keep the batter crisp for a longer
period.) Finally fold in the stiffly whipped egg white. The batter
should be fairly thick in order to coat the fish well. Dip fish pieces in
batter and fry in hot fat for a minute, then lower the heat and fry on
both sides until puffed up and golden in colour.

Serve with tartare sauce.

> *For tartare sauce:*
> ½ cup mayonnaise
> 1 dessertsp. mustard
> 1 dessertsp. chopped capers
> 1 tablesp. chopped pickled gher-
>   kins
> lemon juice to taste

Mix the mustard with lemon juice and stir into the mayonnaise, then
add the chopped gherkins and capers.

Prawn and egg curry
(*Indian*)

20 cooked prawns	2 tomatoes, chopped, or
4 tablesp. oil or ghee	1 dessertsp. tomato purée
1 large chopped onion	1 teasp. salt or to taste
2 cloves garlic, chopped	1 cup thick coconut milk
1 tablesp. curry powder	a few drops lemon juice
2 fresh chillies	3 hard-boiled eggs

Heat the oil in a frying-pan and lightly fry the onion, garlic and
chillies (cut lengthways). Add the curry powder, stir for a minute or
two, add the coconut milk. Simmer gently. Add the cooked prawns,
eggs cut into halves, salt and lemon juice. Stir until the sauce is thick.

Prawns and green peas: Har yun cheng dow
(*Chinese*)

1 lb. prawns	1 cup green peas
1 clove garlic, chopped finely	1 dessertsp. cornflour
1 inch finely chopped fresh ginger	2 tablesp. soya sauce
2 tablesp. oil	½ teasp. sugar

Shell and clean the prawns and remove the black vein. Heat the oil in
a frying-pan, add the chopped garlic and ginger and fry for a minute
or two. Add the prawns and fry until brown, stirring all the time. Add
the peas and their liquor. Mix the cornflour with the soya sauce and
sugar and stir this into the prawns. Cook, stirring continuously, until
the sauce thickens and the prawns are ready.

Sambal goreng Java
(*Indonesian*)

10 oz. small prawns
1 large onion, sliced
4 cloves garlic, chopped
3 red chillies
1 inch fresh ginger, chopped
2 green chillies

3 hard-boiled eggs
1 cup thick coconut milk
½ teasp. sugar
½ teasp. salt
2 tablesp. oil

Wash and clean the prawns. Remove the seeds from the red chillies and soak them in water for 15 minutes to take out the heat, then pound them. Wash and slice the green chillies. Heat the oil in a pan and fry lightly the sliced onion, garlic and ginger. Add the pounded red chillies and prawns and stir well. Add the green chillies and continue frying, stirring all the time. Shell the hard-boiled eggs, cut them into halves and add them to the mixture. Lower the heat, add the coconut milk, season with salt, add the sugar and leave to simmer until prawns are well cooked.

Scandinavian herrings
(*Scandinavian*)

4 large herrings
1 tablesp. mustard
1 tablesp. tomato purée
½ teasp. sugar

2 tablesp. thick cream
salt
pepper

Scale, clean and bone the herrings, leaving the tails on. In a bowl mix the mustard (already made), tomato purée, sugar, cream, salt and pepper. Spread this mixture inside each fish. Roll the herrings, secure with skewers and arrange on a greased ovenproof dish. Dot with butter or brush with melted butter and bake in a moderate oven (350° F., Gas reg. 4) for 30 minutes.

Sole à la meunière
(*French*)

1 sole per person
1 tablesp. milk
½ tablesp. lemon juice
3 tablesp. oil
salt

pepper
Worcestershire sauce
flour for coating
a knob of butter
chopped parsley

Wash fish and remove dark skin but leave on head and tail. In a large deep dish, mix the milk, lemon juice, a few drops of Worcestershire sauce, salt and pepper. Turn fish in this and leave for a few minutes. Take out and coat with flour.

Heat oil in a large frying-pan and when oil is very hot put the fish into it, then reduce the heat a little and fry the sole on both sides until golden brown. Pour off the fat, add the knob of butter and finish cooking in butter. Place the fish on a hot serving dish and garnish with 2 slices of lemon. Sprinkle with a little Worcestershire sauce and chopped parsley. Pour the well-browned butter over all.

Sweet and sour fish
(*Chinese*)

1 whole fish weighing 2 lb.	*For the sauce:*
cornflour	1 cup water
oil for frying	4 tablesp. sugar
	5 tablesp. vinegar
	1 teasp. fresh chopped ginger
	2 teasp. cornflour
	1 tablesp. soya sauce

Scale and clean the fish and make 3 diagonal slashes across it. Dredge it with cornflour. Heat the oil in a large deep frying-pan and holding the fish over the pan, baste the slashes with boiling fat before putting the fish completely into the oil. Fry, turning all the time, for about 15 minutes, or until the fish is cooked through and crisp. Take out and drain. Just before serving, put the fried fish once more into the boiling fat and turn for a minute or two. Drain again. Place on a hot serving dish and pour the sweet and sour sauce over it.

To prepare the sauce: Bring the water, sugar and vinegar to the boil in a saucepan. Add chopped ginger. Blend the cornflour with the soya sauce and add to the hot liquid. Stir over gentle heat until the sauce has thickened.

Trout in wine: Forellen in Wein
(*Swiss*)

4 medium-sized trout	1½ oz. butter
½ pint white wine	1 tablesp. flour
salt	1 tablesp. lemon juice
pepper	1 egg yolk

Clean the fish, sprinkle with salt and pepper and place in a saucepan with the wine. Simmer gently until the fish is tender. Remove from the pan and place on a hot dish. In a separate small saucepan melt the butter, add the flour and cook gently, stirring all the time. Blend in the wine in which the fish was cooked and allow the sauce to thicken. Add the lemon juice and lastly stir in the egg yolk, blended with a little hot sauce. Do not boil after the egg yolk has been added because the sauce might curdle. Pour the sauce over the fish and serve.

Fish with onions
(Turkish)

2 lb. fish, preferably perch	salt
oil for frying	juice of 1 lemon
1 large onion, chopped	black pepper, freshly ground
chopped parsley	

Clean and skin the fish. Cut into slices. Rub with salt and leave to stand for several hours. Heat oil in a frying-pan and fry the slices on a slow heat, turning so that both sides cook evenly. When the fish is done, place it on a hot serving dish and sprinkle with raw chopped onion and parsley. Grind black pepper over the fish and sprinkle with lemon juice.

Meat Dishes

Beef

Beef rendang (*Indonesian*)
Beef rolls (*Polish*)
Beef steaks (*French*)
Beef Stroganoff (*Russian*)
Beef with haricot beans (*Yugoslav*)
Beef with prunes (*Lithuanian*)
Braised sirloin à l'Esterhazy (*Hungarian*)
Cathay steak (*Chinese*)
Fillet steak with Madeira (*Italian*)

Flemish roast (*Belgian*)
Fricco (*Spanish*)
Kaeng Masaman (*Siamese*)
Meat with green sauce (*Persian*)
Pot roast in beer (*German*)
Roast beef à la Radecki (*Polish*)
Schweizer Fleischtopf (*Swiss*)
Stewed sirloin à la Hortobágy (*Hungarian*)
Sukiyaki (*Japanese*)
Wooden Platter Steak (*Hungarian*)

Mutton

Masala chops (*Indian*)
Mutton chops with curd (*Pakastani*)
Mutton roast with curd (*Persian*)

Mutton with cabbage (*Swiss*)
Mutton with spinach (*Pakistani*)
Mutton with vegetables (*Belgian*)
Sheesh kebabs (*Afghanistan*)

Offal

Calf's liver with Madeira (*Polish*)
Fried brains (*Pakistani*)

Liver curry (*Madrasi*)
Veal kidneys (*Italian*)

Pork

Barbecued spare ribs (*Chinese*)
Debrecen pork chops
  (*Hungarian*)
Fragrant pork (*Chinese*)
Fried crisp pork (*Chinese*)
Hochepot à la gantoise (*Belgian*)
Kolozsvar pork cutlets
  (*Hungarian*)

Pork chops with garlic
  (*Czechoslovakian*)
Pork cutlets (*Polish*)
Pork in wine (*French*)
Pork with oranges (*French*)
Viennese roast pork (*Austrian*)

Veal

Boneless birds (*Danish*)
Cutlets of veal à la Perigueux
  (*French*)
Mixed grill (*Italian*)
Lithuanian roast (*Lithuanian*)
Veal cutlets Bolognese (*Italian*)

Veal escalopes (*Swiss*)
Veal escalopes (*Austrian*)
Veal paprikash (*Hungarian*)
Veal 'sparrows' (*Austrian*)
Veal in white sauce (*French*)

MEAT AND COOKING FATS

Roasting, the most popular way of cooking, is also the most expensive as only good cuts of meat can be used for it. Cheaper cuts of meat can be used with excellent results in pot-roasting and braising, a method widely used in Continental and Oriental cookery. This slow way of cooking is done in a deep, covered dish either on top of the stove or in the oven and additional flavour is provided by the use of vegetables, herbs, spices and wine. The advantage of this method is that the dish can be prepared in advance and very often tastes even better when re-heated.

Oil is becoming more widely used in England as the trend grows to cooking with lighter fats. Olive oil or vegetable oil can be used for frying and sautéing almost any kind of meat. A mixture of oil and butter is very satisfactory and prevents the butter from burning. Chinese cooks use lard or vegetable oil such as sesame or peanut oil. Vegetable oils are also used in the Middle East, Pakistan, India and Malaya, but the most popular cooking fat in India and Pakistan is ghee, clarified butter, which does not burn or splatter.

BEEF

Beef rendang
(*Indonesian*)

1 lb. shin or topside beef	2 teasp. salt
6 fresh chillies	2 teasp. sugar
1 inch fresh ginger	3 tablesp. oil
2 onions	½ cup thick coconut milk
3 cloves garlic	water
½ tablesp. tamarind juice, or	
1 tablesp. lemon juice	

Grind the chillies (seeds removed), ginger, onions and garlic together and mix with the meat which has been cut into cubes. Heat the oil in a saucepan and fry the meat cubes for about 5–10 minutes, stirring and turning to brown them on all sides. Add about 1 cup water and allow the contents of the pan to boil for about 20–25 minutes. Add sugar, tamarind or lemon juice and season with salt. Cover pan and cook until meat is tender. Add a little more water if necessary. When the beef is cooked, add the coconut milk and simmer for 5 minutes.

Serve with boiled rice, *see* Section Seven.

Beef rolls: Zrazy zawijane
(*Polish*)

1½ lb. topside beef	salt
2 fairly large onions, sliced	pepper
2 oz. cooking fat	½ lb. fresh mushrooms
2 tablesp. fresh breadcrumbs	1 oz. butter
3 rashers bacon	3–4 tablesp. sour cream
½ oz. dried mushrooms, soaked in	
water	

Cut the beef into six slices (4 oz. each). Flatten with a meat tenderizer which has been dipped in cold water. The slices should be quite thin. Sauté 1 sliced onion in 1 oz. of the hot fat for several minutes until it is transparent. Remove from the heat and add the breadcrumbs. Mix well and divide into six portions. Place the beef slices on a board, season with salt and pepper and place a portion of the fried onion and breadcrumb mixture on each. Cut the bacon into small pieces and cut

up the soaked mushrooms (keeping the water) and put a little of each
on top of the onion and breadcrumb mixture. Roll up the meat slices
and secure with a skewer or thread. Heat the rest of the fat in the
frying-pan, coat the meat rolls with flour and put into the pan. Brown
on all sides. Take out the meat and put it into another pan. Sauté the
second sliced onion in the fat in which the meat has been cooked. Add
it to the meat. Add the water in which the mushrooms have been
soaked and ½ cup hot water to the first pan. Bring to the boil and
scrape well so that all the residue in the pan is mixed with the water.
Pour this over the meat and onions. Cover this pan and put it over the
heat to simmer slowly until the meat is tender and the gravy thick.

Slice the fresh mushrooms, without peeling them. Heat some butter
in a pan and sauté the mushrooms until tender. Season with salt and
pepper and add the sour cream. Stir until well blended and add this to
the meat. Simmer everything for a few minutes, then turn out on to a
dish and serve. Remember to remove the thread if meat rolls were
originally secured in this way.

Beef steaks
(French)

This is how steaks were fried by the chef to Napoleon III: heat a little
butter in a frying-pan and when very hot, place the steaks in the pan.
When the steaks are browned on one side, turn them carefully on to the
other side and sprinkle the brown side with salt. Fry at a fairly high
temperature and when the steaks are brown on both sides remove
them from the pan and place them on a dish on which there are little
pats of butter. There should be one pat of butter to each steak. Press
the steaks lightly with the broad side of a knife and let the juice from
the steaks mix with the butter. Return the steaks to the frying-pan and
fry once more on both sides at a lower temperature. Take out and
place on the dish on which the butter and the meat juices have formed
a gravy. Do not add any more butter.

Beef Stroganoff
(Russian)

1 lb. fillet of beef	salt
1 chopped onion	pepper
½ lb. sliced mushrooms	1 cup sour cream
2 oz. butter	

Cut the meat into finger-long strips. Heat half the butter in a frying-pan and sauté the onion and mushrooms until the mushrooms are cooked. Transfer both the mushrooms and the onions to a saucepan. Add the rest of the butter to the frying-pan and fry the meat for about 5 minutes at a fairly high temperature. Turn frequently to brown on all sides. Add the meat to the saucepan and mix it with the onions and mushrooms. Add the sour cream, bring to the boil and serve.

This dish may be served with fried straw-potatoes.

Beef with haricot beans: Solet
(*Yugoslav*)

2 lb. stewing steak
lard or cooking fat for frying
2 medium-sized onions, thinly sliced
2–3 rashers streaky bacon water

½ lb. haricot beans, soaked in water overnight
salt
pepper
1 teasp. sweet paprika

Heat lard or cooking fat in a saucepan. Add the meat which has been cut into cubes, and brown on all sides. Remove meat from the pan and in the same fat fry the sliced onions until golden in colour. Add the bacon, cut into pieces. Stir for a minute, then return the meat to the pan together with the drained haricot beans. Season with salt and pepper. Add paprika and a little hot water. Cover the pan and cook the meat slowly on a low heat until it is ready. More water can be added if necessary.

Beef with prunes
(*Lithuanian*)

3 lb. brisket of beef
2 onions, sliced
1½ oz. cooking fat
1 lb. dried prunes, soaked in water overnight
1½ cups water

4 cloves
1 small stick cinnamon
1 tablesp. brown sugar
salt
3 tablesp. vinegar

Heat fat in a pan and brown the meat on all sides. Season with salt and add the sliced onions. Continue frying until the onions are golden brown. Add the remaining ingredients, except the prunes. Cover the saucepan and reduce the heat. Simmer slowly for about 1½ hours. Add the prunes. Continue to simmer for a further 1½ hours, or until meat is tender.

Braised sirloin à l'Esterhazy: Eszterházi rostélyos
(*Hungarian*)

6 sirloin steaks, 1 inch thick
1 onion, sliced
1 carrot, cut in thin strips
2 stalks celery, cut in thin strips
1 parsnip, cut in pieces
3–4 oz. fat for frying

a few peppercorns
1 teasp. paprika
salt to taste
a few capers
½ cup sour cream or thick fresh cream

Beat the steaks with a mallet. Heat fat in a pan. Put in meat and brown on both sides. Remove meat from pan. Put the vegetables in the pan. Sprinkle with flour and sauté lightly for a few minutes. Add a little water. Return the meat to the pan, add salt, peppercorns and paprika, cover the pan and cook slowly on a low heat until the meat is tender. When the meat is cooked, place it on a hot dish.
To prepare the sauce: Add capers to the gravy, stir in sour cream or cream, bring to boil and pour over the steaks. Serve with noodles, gnocchi or rice.

Cathay steak
(*Chinese*)

1 lb. fillet steak
1 teasp. sugar
1 teasp. ve-tsin (monosodium glutamate)
1 inch fresh ginger, crushed

1 clove garlic, crushed
2 tablesp. soya sauce
½ teasp. salt
4 tablesp. oil

Cut the beef into slices ⅓ inch thick and place in a bowl containing the sugar, ve-tsin, ginger, garlic, soya sauce and salt. Leave the beef slices to stand in this mixture for at least 1 hour. Heat a pan, add the oil and when this is very hot, fry the steaks over a fairly high heat until they are well seared all over. Serve the steaks with the juices from the pan poured over them.

Fillet steak with Madeira: Filetto al Madera
(*Italian*)

4 fillet steaks, 1 inch thick
2 rashers bacon
1 small onion, sliced
salt

pepper
1 oz. butter
¼ cup hot beef stock
½ cup Madeira

Heat the fat in a pan. Fry the rashers of bacon, remove them from the pan and dice them. Put the onion in the fat in which the bacon was fried, and sauté until it is golden in colour. Remove from the pan. Increase the heat and fry the fillet steaks for 2 minutes on each side. Season them with salt and pepper and add the melted butter, the hot stock and the Madeira. Cook over a moderate heat for 2 minutes on each side and remove from the pan to a serving dish. Serve with the juices from the pan poured over the steaks and garnish with the diced bacon.

Flemish roast
(*Belgian*)

3 lb. beef (topside, silverside or rump)	½ lb. cooked gammon
1 large onion, sliced	1 savoy cabbage
1 diced carrot	salt
1 celery stalk, cut in pieces	pepper
	lard for frying

Heat lard in a large pan. Wipe meat with a damp cloth and put into the hot fat. Brown on all sides. Season with salt and pepper and add onion, carrot and celery and a little water. Cover pan and simmer on a low heat. Meanwhile parboil the cabbage in another saucepan and cut it into four pieces. Add the gammon and the cabbage to the meat when it is nearly cooked and allow all to cook until the meat and cabbage are tender. Remove the meat and slice it. Place it on a hot dish and surround it with the cabbage and the gammon which should now be cut into strips. Pass the liquid from the meat pan through a sieve and pour it over meat.

Serve with boiled potatoes.

Fricco
(*Spanish*)

1 lb. stewing steak	cayenne pepper
2 medium-sized onions, chopped	2 lb. potatoes
2 oz. butter or cooking fat	¼ pint sour cream
salt	chopped parsley

Heat the fat in a pan with a thick base. Cut the meat into cubes and brown in the hot fat. Remove from the pan. Sauté the chopped onions in the same fat. In a heavy saucepan arrange the meat cubes, add the onion and a little water. Cover the pan and simmer on a low heat until half-cooked. Remove the meat from the pan. Peel and roughly slice the potatoes. Arrange a layer of potatoes on the bottom of the pan, then a layer of meat and so on until all the meat and potatoes have been used up, finishing with a layer of potatoes. Season with salt and pepper. Add more water if necessary and simmer until the meat is tender and the potatoes done. Add the sour cream and simmer for a few minutes longer. Before serving sprinkle with chopped parsley.

Note: Mutton or pork may be substituted for the beef in this recipe.

Kaeng Masaman
(*Siamese*)

2 lb. stewing beef	2 cardamoms
2 tablesp. oil	1 teasp. salt
1 onion, chopped finely	2 oz. roasted peanuts
5 cloves garlic, chopped	1 tablesp. soya sauce
1 inch fresh ginger, chopped	1 tablesp. vinegar
6 cloves	2 cups coconut milk
1 stick cinnamon	1 onion, sliced thinly and fried
½ teasp. red chilli powder	until crisp
½ teasp. sugar	

Cube the meat or cut it into finger-length pieces. Put into a pan and cover with water. Cook until half done. Take out meat from pan and keep liquid. Heat the oil in another pan and sauté the chopped onion until transparent. Add garlic and fry for a minute. Add the meat pieces, ginger, cloves, cinnamon, sugar, cardamoms, red chilli, salt, peanuts, soya sauce and vinegar. Stir and add coconut milk. Cover the pan and simmer gently for about an hour, or until the meat is tender. Add stock from time to time as necessary. Pour out on to a serving dish and garnish with crisply fried onion.

Serve with rice and sliced cucumber which has been soaked in salt and vinegar.

Meat with green sauce: Khoresh Qormeh sabzi
(*Persian*)

1 lb. stewing beef	*For the sauce:*
5 tablesp. oil	½ small onion, chopped
1 large onion, chopped	2 tablesp. chopped parsley
4 oz. dried kidney beans	1 teasp. fenugreek
1 teasp. salt	1 teasp. turmeric powder
2 cups hot water	½ teasp. cinnamon
	2 tablesp. lemon juice

Heat 3 tablespoons oil in a pan and sauté lightly the chopped onion. Add the meat, cut into cubes, and fry, stirring constantly until the meat has browned. Cover with about 2 cups hot water. Add the beans, season with salt, and cook gently with the lid on over a low heat for about an hour.

To prepare the sauce: In a separate saucepan put the remaining oil and heat. Sauté the onion. Add parsley and spices and fry until the mixture has changed colour.

Add the meat to the sauce and continue simmering until the meat is tender. Add the lemon juice and simmer for a further 10 minutes.

Serve with boiled rice, *see* Section Seven.

Pot roast in beer: Rindfleisch in bier gedampft
(German)

3 lb. topside or silverside beef	3 tablesp. vinegar
2 teasp. salt	1 tablesp. brown syrup
1 large onion, sliced	beer and water in equal quantities
1 carrot, diced	(see recipe)
2 cloves	3–4 slices fat bacon
1 bay leaf	1 tablesp. flour
6 peppercorns	

Place the meat in an earthenware bowl and add salt, onion, carrot, cloves, bay leaf, peppercorns, syrup and vinegar. Add enough beer and water to come half-way up the bowl. Leave to marinate for several hours or overnight, if possible. Remove meat from the marinade. Heat a little fat in a large heavy pan and put the meat into it. Brown it on all sides. Add the bacon and the marinade. Cover pan and simmer slowly on a low heat for about 3 hours, or until the meat is tender. Remove meat and strain rest of mixture through a sieve into another pan. Mix some flour with a little of the liquid in the first pan. Add the rest of the liquid. Bring to the boil and simmer for a few minutes. Put meat and strained vegetables on a serving dish and pour sauce over these.

Roast beef à la radecki
(Polish)

2–3 lb. sirloin beef	1 teasp. sugar
3 oz. butter or cooking fat	2 egg yolks
3 tablesp. grated horseradish	1 teasp. lemon juice
salt	2 tablesp. thick cream
pepper	1 teasp. flour
1 tablesp. fresh breadcrumbs	water

F

Heat 2 oz. butter or cooking fat in a pan and brown meat in it on all sides. Season with salt and pepper and add a little hot water. Cover the pan and pot-roast the meat until quite tender. Take meat out of pan, put it on a board and cut the meat once lengthways, BUT DO NOT CUT IT RIGHT THROUGH.

Mix the horseradish with 1 oz. softened butter, breadcrumbs, egg yolks, sugar, lemon juice and salt. Mix well and put mixture in the cut in the meat. Press meat tightly and secure with string. Return meat to pan and simmer for 30 minutes. Add cream blended with flour, and cook for a few minutes longer until the gravy is thick and golden in colour.

Schweizer Fleischtopf
(Swiss)

1 lb. stewing steak	1 teasp. paprika
1 lb. shoulder pork	¼ teasp. marjoram
1 large onion, sliced	1 wine glass white wine
2 tablesp. oil	2 lb. potatoes
salt	1 lb. tomatoes
6 oz. bacon, diced	water

Cut up the meat into cubes. Heat the oil in a pan and brown the meat and bacon on all sides. Remove all meat from the pan and sauté the onion in the fat until transparent but not brown. Return the meat to the pan, season with salt and add paprika, marjoram, wine and a little hot water. Cover the pan and simmer on a low heat for about 2 hours. Peel and slice the potatoes and the tomatoes. Add them to the meat and continue cooking for 30 minutes or until the meat is tender and the potatoes cooked.

Stewed sirloin à la Hortobágy: Hortobágyi rostélyos
(Hungarian)

6 sirloin steaks (each weighing about 6 oz.)	1 dessertsp. paprika
	1 large green pepper
2 teasp. salt	3 tomatoes
1 oz. flour	caraway seeds (optional)
4 oz. lard or any cooking fat	pinch marjoram
2 medium-sized onions, chopped	stock or water

Heat fat in a pan. Sprinkle the steaks with salt, roll in flour and fry in the hot fat on both sides. Remove meat from the pan and transfer to a casserole or a stewing pan. In the same fat in which the steaks were fried, sauté the onions until golden brown. Add paprika, caraway seeds, marjoram and a little stock or water. Bring to boil. Pour over the steaks. Cover casserole or pan and cook slowly either in the oven or on a low heat on the top of the cooker. Add a little more water or stock if necessary. When the steaks are nearly done, add the green pepper (cut into large pieces) and the tomatoes (sliced). Continue cooking until the vegetables are cooked and the meat tender. Serve with semolina dumplings, *see* Section Seven. Place one dumpling on each steak.

Sukiyaki
(*Japanese*)

1 lb. fillet beef, sliced thinly	*For the sauce:*
2 large onions, sliced	¼ cup soya sauce
8 oz. bamboo shoots, shredded	½ cup water
12 mushrooms	2 tablesp. sarké or dry white
6 spring onions, cut into pieces	wine
2 inches long	2 tablesp. sugar
8 oz. cabbage, shredded	
1 piece of beef suet	
4 oz. of fine vermicelli, boiled	
4 eggs	

To prepare the sukiyaki: Heat a large chafing dish and grease it with a piece of suet. Brown the meat pieces slightly and start to add the cut vegetables in the following order: onions, bamboo shoots, mushrooms, cabbage.

Keep turning so that everything browns evenly. Moisten with the sauce and add the vermicelli. Cook for 10–15 minutes.

To prepare the sauce: Boil all ingredients in a small saucepan for a few minutes.

Prepare the sukiyaki at the table and serve each guest with a small bowl in which a raw egg is broken and topped with the sukiyaki.

Serve boiled rice in a separate bowl.

Wooden Platter Steak: Fatáneyros
(*Hungarian*)

The name derives from olden times, when the wooden platter was simply a piece of wood cut from a tree trunk and used as a plate at picnics. The dish is like a mixed grill and consists of different kinds of meat, such as slices of fillet of beef, tender pork cutlets, sliced goose liver and slices of bacon, grilled or roasted on a spit. Serve on a big wooden platter with a heap of fried potatoes in the middle. Garnish with green peppers cut into slices, cucumbers and beetroot.

MUTTON

Masala chops
(Indian)

	For the masala:
1 lb. lamb or mutton chops	1 inch fresh ginger
1 lb. potatoes	5 red chillies
1 cup tomato purée	5 cloves garlic
ghee or oil for frying	1 teasp. mustard
2 large onions, sliced	1 teasp. cumin seeds
chopped coriander leaves	½ teasp. turmeric powder
tomatoes	salt
green pepper	vinegar

To prepare the masala: Grind all the ingredients and mix with a little vinegar into a paste.

Flatten the chops by beating them lightly. Peel and slice the potatoes thickly. Rub the masala on to the chops and the potatoes, season with salt and leave for a few hours.

Heat the fat in a pan and fry the chops till evenly browned on both sides. Add the tomato purée. Cover the pan and simmer until there is little liquid left and the meat is tender. Arrange chops in a greased ovenproof dish.

Heat some oil or ghee in a pan and fry the potatoes until crisp. Remove and drain and put them on top of the chops in the dish, and keep the dish warm.

Again heat some oil or ghee in a pan and brown the onion slices. When ready, add these to the ovenproof dish. Put dish under the grill for 5 minutes before serving. Garnish with tomato slices, green pepper rings and coriander leaves.

Mutton chops with curd: Dhai chop masala
(Pakistani)

1 lb. mutton chops	½ teasp. cumin powder
1 large onion, chopped	1 stick cinnamon
2 tomatoes, sliced	2–3 cloves
3 green chillies, sliced	½ cup curd or yoghurt
salt	a few peppercorns
½ teasp. coriander powder	oil or ghee for frying

Wipe the chops with a damp cloth and trim off the fat. Heat the oil or ghee in a pan and sauté lightly the chopped onion. Add the tomatoes, chillies, salt, coriander, cumin powder, peppercorns, stick of cinnamon and cloves, and pour over the yoghurt or curd. Place the chops on top, seal the pan well and cook on a medium heat for an hour. Take off the lid and cook for a few minutes till the fat floats to the top.

Mutton roast with curd
(*Persian*)

3 lb. leg of mutton	1 teasp. cumin seeds
6 cloves garlic	½ teasp. powdered turmeric
1 inch fresh ginger	1½ cups curd or yoghurt
4 red chillies	salt

Wash the meat and prick all over with a fork or skewer. Grind garlic, ginger, red chillies and cumin seeds into a paste and mix in the powdered turmeric. Sprinkle salt over the meat and rub the paste well in. Put meat into a dish, cover with curd or yoghurt and leave in a cold place for twenty-four hours. Turn the meat now and again to allow for the equal distribution of the spices. Roast in a pre-heated oven (400° F., Gas reg. 6) for about 1½ hours, or until meat is well cooked and the gravy sizzling and rich.

Mutton with cabbage: Schaffleisch mit Kabis
(*Swiss*)

1½ lb. shoulder or neck mutton	salt
1 lb. savoy cabbage, shredded	pepper
1 lb. potatoes, peeled and cubed	2 oz. lard for frying
2 onions, chopped	hot water
1 clove garlic	

Cut the meat into cubes. Heat the fat in a large saucepan and put in the meat. Brown on all sides. Add the onions and crushed garlic clove and turn. Season with salt and pepper and add the coarsely shredded cabbage and potatoes. Mix well and add ¾ pint of hot water. Cover the pan and simmer on a low heat for 1½–2 hours, or until the meat is tender. Add more water during the cooking, if necessary.

Mutton with spinach: Sag gosht
(Pakistani)

2 lb. shoulder or leg mutton	1 dessertsp. garam masala
1 lb. spinach	1 teasp. chilli powder
4 oz. ghee or oil	1 bay leaf
3 large onions, chopped	4 oz. sour milk or yoghurt
4 cloves garlic	salt
1 inch fresh ginger, chopped	hot water

Wash the spinach, remove the stalks and chop very finely. Cut the meat into cubes. Heat the ghee or oil in a pan and sauté lightly the chopped onions. Add the crushed garlic, ginger, garam masala, chilli powder and bay leaf. Continue frying for a few minutes. Add the meat and stir until brown on all sides. Add the spinach and salt and a little hot water. Cover the pan and simmer on a low heat until the meat is nearly done. Add the sour milk or yoghurt and continue cooking until the meat is tender and the gravy thick and rich. Add more water during the cooking, if necessary.

Mutton with vegetables: Navarin aux legumes
(Belgian)

2 lb. shoulder or leg of mutton	2 tablesp. tomato purée
salt	bouquet garni
pepper	6 oz. carrots
½ teasp. sugar	6 oz. turnips
2 oz. cooking fat	12 shallots
1 tablesp. flour	water
1 clove garlic	

Cut the meat into cubes and season with salt and pepper. Sprinkle with sugar. Melt half the fat in a pan and when hot, put in the meat and brown on all sides. Drain off the fat and sprinkle the meat with flour. Cook for a few minutes, stirring all the time. Add the crushed garlic and tomato purée. Stir again. Add hot water and bouquet garni. Cover and simmer on a low heat for 1 hour. (Take care not to have too much liquid, though if necessary water can be added whilst meat is simmering.)

When the meat has cooked for 1 hour, heat the rest of the fat in another pan and toss the shallots and other vegetables in this. Add vegetables to meat. Cover the pan again and simmer for 1 hour longer.

Sheesh kebabs
(*Afghanistan*)

1 lb. leg mutton	8 oz. dumba (*see* Note)
1 cup curd or yoghurt	small onions or wedges of onion
5 cloves garlic	tomatoes cut into cubes
salt	green chillies
black pepper	lime juice

Crush the garlic and mix with the curd or yoghurt. Season with salt and pepper. Cut meat into 1 inch cubes. Put meat and cubed dumba in a large bowl and marinade in the curd mixture for at least 2 hours. Prepare metal skewers: place a cube of meat on the skewer, then a cube of dumba, a small onion and a tomato quarter. Repeat until the skewer is filled. Brown meat on skewer over a charcoal fire or under a grill for about 10 minutes. Remove from heat, sprinkle with lemon juice and leave for 30 minutes. Return skewer to fire or grill and cook for 10 minutes longer. Serve garnished with lemon slices and green chillies.

Note: Dumba is the fat from a sheep's tail. When this is not available omit it and baste the meat while it is grilling with melted fat.

OFFAL

Calf's liver with Madeira
(*Polish*)

	For sauce:
1 calf's liver	1 oz. butter
salt pork fat for larding	1 oz. flour
flour	½ pint stock
salt	½ teasp. sugar
pepper	½ teasp. caramel
butter for frying	juice of ½ lemon
milk or	a few mushrooms
milk and water	4 tablesp. Madeira

Skin the liver and leave it to soak for several hours in milk or milk and water. Take out, dry and lard with pork fat which has been cut into long narrow strips. Slice the larded liver, dust with flour, season with salt and pepper. Heat butter in a pan and fry liver slices on both sides. Pour the prepared Madeira sauce into the pan and cook the liver for 3–4 minutes more. If the sauce is too thick, add a little stock. *To prepare the sauce:* Make a roux from the butter and flour and add the stock gently. Cook slowly, stirring until the sauce thickens. Add sugar, caramel, lemon juice and Madeira. Bring to boil and strain sauce through a sieve. Add cooked sliced mushrooms and mix well.

Fried brains: Bhoona bheja
(*Pakistani*)

1 sheep's brain	3 tablesp. ghee or oil
1 large onion, chopped	1 teasp. salt
1 inch fresh ginger, finely chopped	1 tablesp. fresh coriander leaves,
2 cloves garlic	chopped

Clean the brain, leaving it whole. Heat the oil or ghee in a pan and sauté the onion lightly. When it is golden in colour, add the ginger and garlic and fry for a few minutes. Place the brain carefully in the pan, season with salt and cook for a few minutes. Turn carefully and continue cooking until the brain is cooked and well browned. Sprinkle with coriander leaves and serve.

Liver curry: Kaleji
(*Madrasi*)

1 lb. sheep's liver
4 tablesp. ghee or oil
1 large onion, chopped
3 cloves garlic, crushed
2 red chillies, cut into pieces
½ teasp. red chilli powder

½ teasp. garam masala
2 ripe tomatoes, cut in quarters
8 oz. green peas (cooked)
salt
1½ cup thick coconut milk

Cut the liver into 1 inch cubes. Heat the oil in a pan and fry the chopped onion lightly. Add the garlic, red chillies, chilli powder and garam masala. Stir for a few minutes. Add the tomatoes, liver and peas. Season with salt, lower the heat and simmer gently for about 10 minutes. Cover the pan during this time. Add the coconut milk. Cover the pan again and cook until the liver is tender and the gravy thick and rich.

Serve with boiled rice, *see* Section Seven.

Veal kidneys: Rognoni saltati
(*Italian*)

4 kidneys
2 tablesp. oil
salt
pepper

¼ teasp. lemon rind
4 tablesp. Marsala or white wine
2 tablesp. tomato purée
2 tablesp. chopped parsley

Skin and core the kidneys and put them in boiling water for a minute or two. Drain them and pat dry on a kitchen towel. Cut them into slices, dust with flour. Heat the oil in a pan and fry the kidneys over a moderate heat for about 5 minutes. Season with salt and pepper and add the lemon rind. Add the wine and boil liquid until it is reduced to half its volume. Add the tomato purée and a few drops of water. Heat this quickly and turn out onto a serving dish. Garnish with chopped parsley.

PORK

Barbecued spare ribs
(*Chinese*)

2 lb. pork spare ribs	1 tablesp. wine or sherry
2 cloves garlic	1 tablesp. sugar
1 inch fresh ginger, chopped	½ teasp. salt
3 tablesp. soya sauce	½ tablesp. 'five spice powder'

Mix together the crushed garlic, ginger, soya sauce, wine or sherry, sugar and spice powder. Place meat in a bowl, sprinkle with salt and rub well with the mixed ingredients. Leave for several hours.

Put pork in a greased roasting dish. Slice meat between the bones, but not quite through. Brush skin with vinegar and put in a pre-heated oven. Cook at 425° F., Gas reg. 7 for 20 minutes, then reduce to a moderate heat and cook for another hour or until the meat is ready. Divide spare ribs and serve.

Debrecen pork chops: Debreceni sertés karaj
(*Hungarian*)

6 pork chops	1 green pepper
1 large onion, chopped	2 medium-sized tomatoes
salt	2 oz. bacon, cut in cubes
paprika	4 oz. Debrecen sausage or a
lard for frying	Continental sausage

Heat lard in a frying-pan. Brown chops in lard. Remove and place in a heavy pan. Fry chopped onion in lard. Cut the green peppers and slice the tomatoes and add to the pork chops, together with the onion. Season with salt and paprika. Add a little water. Cover the pan and simmer on a low heat until meat is nearly cooked.

Heat some more lard in a frying-pan. Fry the cubed bacon for a few minutes. Add the sliced sausage and stir. Add bacon and sausage to chops and continue cooking until meat is tender.

Fragrant pork: Chiang jou
(*Chinese*)

2 lb. tender loin of pork	½ teasp. aniseed
4 tablesp. sugar	8 cloves
1½ cup wine or sherry	1 stick cinnamon
⅓ cup soya sauce	1 teasp. salt
water	peel from 1 orange, dried

Cut the pork into several big chunks and place in a saucepan with all the other ingredients. Add a little water, cover the pan and boil for 3 hours. Add just enough water during the cooking time to prevent the meat and other ingredients from burning. Keep the heat moderately high so that the meat juices will not escape. When the meat is cooked remove it from the saucepan, cut it into 1½-inch cubes and serve with the sauce.

Fried crisp pork: Jee jou juk
(*Chinese*)

1 lb. belly pork	a pinch of 'five spice powder'
3 tablesp. soya sauce	
1 tablesp. sherry or wine	*For batter:*
oil or lard for frying	1 egg
stock or water	3 tablesp. cornflour
1 tablesp. sugar	

Put the pork in a saucepan. Add soya sauce, wine or sherry, sugar and spice powder. Cover with 2 cups stock or water and simmer until tender. Remove meat from saucepan and cool. When cool, cut into small cubes, about 1 × 1½ inches and dip in a batter. Heat oil or lard in a deep frying-pan and fry cubes coated in batter until golden brown in colour and crisp.
To make batter: Mix cornflour and 1 beaten egg together.

Hochepot à la gantoise
(*Belgian*)

2 lb gammon	4 diced carrots
salt	2 turnips, cut in pieces
1 bay leaf	1 small savoy cabbage
thyme	3 potatoes, peeled and cubed
water	

Put the meat in a saucepan. Add salt, bay leaf and thyme. Cover with water and bring to the boil. Add carrots and turnips. Cook for 1 hour and add the cabbage cut into quarters. (If there is too much liquid in the pan, take out the meat and reduce stock by rapid boiling; return meat to the saucepan.) Cover the saucepan and continue cooking for a while before adding the potatoes. Cook until the meat is tender and the vegetables ready. Serve the meat on a dish, surrounded by the vegetables.

Kolozsvar pork cutlets: Kolozsvari sertés karaj
(Hungarian)

6 pork chops	6 oz. streaky bacon or gammon,
1 large onion, chopped	cubed
1 oz. lard	1 lb. sauerkraut
salt	2 tablesp. sour cream
paprika	hot water
2 tablesp. tomato purée	

Heat lard in saucepan. Fry the chopped onion until golden in colour. Add tomato purée, salt, paprika and a little hot water. Bring to the boil and cook for a few minutes. Add the chops. Cover the pan and simmer on a low heat. When chops are half-cooked, put in bacon or gammon and the sauerkraut. Cook until chops are tender. Add sour cream and serve.

Pork chops with garlic
(Czechoslovakian)

4 pork chops	pepper
3 cloves garlic	lard for frying
salt	

Chop garlic very finely, then crush it with salt to make a paste. Spread the chops with the paste. Add more salt if necessary and sprinkle with pepper.

Heat the lard in a frying-pan. Put in chops and fry on both sides. Reduce heat and continue frying over a moderate heat until meat is tender. Serve hot or cold.

Pork cutlets: Kotlety schabowe
(*Polish*)

4 pork chops	1 egg
salt	dried breadcrumbs
pepper	lard for frying
flour	

Trim the chops, cutting off surplus fat. Beat meat with a tenderizer.
Make a few incisions around the edges of the chop. Season with salt
and pepper, dip in flour then in beaten egg which has been mixed
with a teaspoon of water. Coat the chops with breadcrumbs, press
down the coating. Heat fat in a frying-pan. Put in chops and fry on
both sides until golden brown and cooked through.

Serve with sauerkraut or boiled cabbage.

Pork in wine: Porc au vin
(*French*)

4 pork chops	a few peppercorns
salt	1 onion
pepper	1 clove
1½ cups dry white wine	fat for roasting
1 small bay leaf	

Put the chops in a bowl, sprinkle with salt and pour wine over them.
Add the bay leaf, peppercorns, and onion stuck with clove. Leave to
stand for several hours. Remove chops from marinade and dry. Heat
the fat in a roasting pan and place the chops in it. Pre-heat the oven
to 425° F., Gas reg. 7 and roast the chops, basting with the fat, for
about 10 minutes. Add ½ cup of the marinade and the onion and
continue cooking and basting until the meat is tender. Add more of
the marinade if necessary.

Pork with oranges: Porc à l'orange
(*French*)

3–4 lb. loin of pork	2 cloves
½ wine glass brandy	bouquet garni
1 oz. lard	salt
1 large onion, sliced	½ cup dry white wine
2 carrots	1 orange
veal knuckle	

Heat the fat in a frying-pan. Put the pork in and brown it on all sides. Pour the brandy over the meat and flame it. Transfer the pork to a heavy pan. Fry onion in the frying-pan. Add onion and carrots to the meat, together with the veal knuckle, cloves and bouquet garni. Pour the wine over the meat, season with salt. Cover pan and simmer slowly on top of the stove for about 2 hours. (If needed, a little water can be added during this time.)

Skin the orange and squeeze out the juice. Cut the skin into very thin strips and boil until soft. Drain.

Remove the cooked meat to a hot serving dish and keep warm whilst preparing the sauce. Pour sauce over meat and serve.

To prepare the sauce: Strain the liquid from the pork through a damp cloth into a bowl, add the orange juice and the orange skin. Return all to the pan. Bring to the boil and pour over the meat.

Viennese roast pork: Schweinscarre
(*Austrian*)

3 lb. loin of pork	caraway seeds
1½ cups vinegar	1 large onion, sliced
salt	1 teasp. flour

Pound meat with a tenderizer. Put it in a dish and pour boiling vinegar over it. Leave for 2 hours. Take out the meat from the marinade, dry it and rub it with salt. Sprinkle it with caraway seeds. Grease a roasting tin and put the meat into it. Pre-heat the oven to 425° F., Gas reg. 7 and roast meat for about 20 minutes, reduce the heat to 375° F., Gas reg. 4. When the meat has changed colour, add sliced onion and sprinkle with flour. Continue cooking for 1–1½ hours (basting frequently) until the meat is brown and tender. When the meat is cooked, remove from the tin to a hot serving dish. Remove excess fat from gravy, slice the meat and pour the gravy over it.

Serve with cabbage and boiled potatoes.

VEAL

Boneless birds
(Danish)

2 thin slices leg of veal per
person
bacon rashers
chopped parsley
water

salt
pepper
flour
butter for frying

The slices of veal should be about 4 × 5 inches. Pound the meat until very thin and season with salt and pepper. On each slice place a rasher of bacon and 1 teaspoon of chopped parsley. Roll tightly and secure with toothpicks or a piece of thin string. Dip in flour. Heat the fat in a pan and put the veal rolls in the hot fat. Brown on all sides. Add enough hot water to cover the bottom of the frying-pan and simmer the meat slowly until tender. Add a little more water during cooking, if necessary. Serve with potato purée.

Cutlets of veal à la Perigueux
(French)

1 slice of veal fillet per person
pâté de foie gras
1–2 eggs
flour

dried breadcrumbs
salt
pepper
butter and oil for frying

Flatten out the slices of veal until they are as thin as possible and measure about 4 × 8 inches. Sprinkle with salt and pepper and put some of the pâté on one half of each slice. Spread fairly thickly and evenly without covering the edges. Fold the slices over and form into cutlets, securing the edges (by hitting them with a mallet). Place a small piece of veal rib-bone on every cutlet to form a 'handle'. Roll the cutlets in flour, dip them in beaten egg and lastly roll them in breadcrumbs. Heat the oil and butter in a frying-pan and fry the cutlets over a low heat for about 10 minutes. Turn them once.

Serve with button mushrooms, cooked in butter, and green peas.

Mixed grill: Fritto misto
(Italian)

4 small veal or lamb cutlets	2 oz. mushrooms
1 calf's brain or lamb's sweet-	salt
bread	pepper
2 cloves garlic	2 eggs
2 aubergines	flour
2 artichokes (optional)	2 cups olive oil

Rub the meat with the chopped garlic. Clean the brains, boil them for 5 minutes in salt water, drain and cut into four pieces. Peel the aubergines, slice thinly and sprinkle with salt and pepper. (If using artichokes, take only the base of very young artichokes.) Beat the eggs with a little salt and dip the meat, brains, aubergines, mushrooms and artichokes (if used) in the egg. Roll in flour. Heat oil in a deep frying-pan until the blue smoke is rising. Fry everything in it. Drain and serve immediately.

Lithuanian roast
(Lithuanian)

3 lb. veal (leg, shoulder or loin)	salt
2 carrots, grated	pepper
2 stalks celery, grated	6 oz. salt pork fat for larding
1 large onion, grated	2 oz. cooking fat
1 tablesp. finely chopped parsley	4 tablesp. sour cream
2 tablesp. mustard (powder)	

Wipe the meat with a damp cloth and rub well with a mixture of grated carrots, celery, onion, parsley and mustard. Place the meat in a bowl and press down with a lid. Leave in a cool place for a day or two. Take out and lard with the salt pork fat, cut into long strips. Season with salt and pepper and dust with flour.

Place the meat in a roasting pan with the cooking fat and put in a pre-heated oven (425° F., Gas reg. 7). Roast for 15 minutes. Reduce the heat to 325° F., Gas reg. 3. Add the meat juice left in the bowl in which the meat was kept and baste the veal frequently with the fat and the juice in the pan. Roast for about 2 hours or until the meat is tender.

Mix the sour cream with a little of the juice from the meat, and add to the pan before serving.

Veal cutlets Bolognese
(*Italian*)

4 slices fillet of veal	dried breadcrumbs
4 thin slices of raw proscuitto ham	salt
	pepper
1 beaten egg	butter for frying
4 tablesp. Parmesan cheese	

Flatten the veal slices, season with salt and pepper and dip into beaten egg, then coat with breadcrumbs. Heat the butter in a frying-pan and fry the cutlets over a low heat, turning once. When the meat is golden in colour, place a slice of ham, cut to the same size as the cutlet, on top of each and sprinkle each with 1 tablespoon of grated Parmesan cheese. Grease a shallow dish and place the cutlets in it. Bake in a pre-heated oven or put under the grill until the cheese has melted.

Veal escalopes: Schweizer Kalbsschnitzel
(*Swiss*)

4 slices fillet of veal	pepper
5 oz. mushrooms	4 tablesp. white wine
2 oz. butter	1 tablesp. tomato purée
salt	1 tablesp. chopped parsley

Flatten the veal slices and season with salt and pepper. Slice the mushrooms. Heat the butter in a frying-pan and fry the veal slices. Remove the meat from the pan and keep hot. Sauté the mushrooms in the pan, add the wine and tomato purée. Return the meat to the pan and cook for a few minutes longer, until the meat is cooked. Place the veal on a hot dish, sprinkle with chopped parsley and put the mushrooms on top. Pour the gravy over the meat.

Serve with grilled tomatoes and potato purée.

Veal escalopes: Wiener Schnitzel
(*Austrian*)

1 slice fillet of veal per person (4 oz.)	*For garnish:*
salt	1 fried egg per person
lemon juice	fillets of anchovy
flour	wedges of lemon
dried breadcrumbs	
1 egg	
butter and oil for frying	

G

Flatten the escalopes with a mallet. Sprinkle with salt and a few drops of lemon juice. Dust with flour, dip in the beaten egg and finally coat in breadcrumbs. Heat a liberal amount of oil and butter in a frying-pan and fry escalopes in it for about 5 minutes on each side.

Serve with a fried egg on top of each one, garnished with a fillet of anchovy and a slice of lemon.

Veal paprikash: Borjú pörkölt
(Hungarian)

2 lb. shoulder of veal	1 green pepper
2 oz. lard or cooking fat	2 tomatoes
1 large onion, chopped	salt
a few drops of garlic juice (op-	2 tablesp. sour cream
tional)	1 tablesp. flour
2 teasp. sweet paprika	

Cut the meat into cubes and chop the onion. Heat the fat in a pan and sauté the onion lightly. Add the meat and brown all over, turning frequently. Add the garlic juice (if used). Slice the pepper and the tomatoes and add to the meat. Sprinkle with paprika and salt, and add about 2–3 tablespoons water. Cover the pan and simmer the meat over a low heat until tender (about 45 minutes). Stir the flour into the sour cream and add this to the meat towards the end of the cooking time. Serve with gnocchi (*see* Section Seven).

Veal 'sparrows': Kalbsvogerln
(Austrian)

6 slices fillet of veal	2 tablesp. Madeira
8 oz. mushrooms	salt
1 slice white bread soaked in milk	pepper
and squeezed	1 oz. butter
1 egg yolk	flour
2 oz. butter	2 tablesp. thick cream
stock or water	1 piece lemon

Flatten the veal fillets, sprinkle with salt and rub with a piece of lemon rind. Chop the mushrooms. Heat the butter in a pan and sauté the mushrooms for a few minutes. Mix with soaked bread, egg yolk and Madeira. Season with salt and pepper. Remove from pan and divide mixture into six portions. Place a portion on each of the veal slices. Roll the slices and secure with toothpicks or thread. Roll the slices in flour and put them in the pan containing the hot fat. Brown them in the butter, then place them in a warmed casserole or pan. Pour a little stock or water into the frying-pan in which the rolls were fried. Bring to the boil, stirring to loosen residue in pan, and make it into a gravy. Pour over the meat in the casserole or pan. Cover and cook in a moderate oven or over a slow heat on the top of the stove until the meat is tender. (About 45 minutes.) Just before serving, add the cream and bring to the boil.

Serve with noodles or macaroni.

Veal in white sauce: Blanquette de veau
(*French*)

2 lb. breast veal	10 shallots
1 onion	6 oz. mushrooms, sliced
1 carrot, sliced	1 oz. flour
sprig parsley	1 egg yolk
a few peppercorns	2 tablesp. cream
bouquet garni	1 teasp. lemon juice
2 teasp. salt	salt
2 oz. butter	pepper
water	

Cut the meat in cubes and place in a saucepan. Cover with cold water and bring slowly to the boil. Skim well. Add 1 onion, the carrot, parsley, peppercorns, and the bouquet garni. Season with salt and simmer for about 1¼ hours or until the veal is tender. Cover the pan during this time. Remove the meat from the pan when it is cooked and strain the stock.

Heat 1 oz. of butter in a frying-pan and sauté the shallots and the sliced mushrooms in it. Cover the pan and steam the onions and mushrooms until tender. Add a little water, if necessary. Season with salt and pepper.

Melt 1 oz. butter in another pan and stir in the flour. Gradually add the strained stock, mixing it to a smooth sauce. (About 1 pint of stock will be needed.) Add the meat, onions and mushrooms to the sauce and simmer gently for another 5 minutes. Add the cream mixed with the egg yolk and stir until the sauce thickens. Do not boil. Add the lemon juice. Serve on a hot platter surrounded by boiled rice.

Minced Meat Dishes

(including mince with vegetables and pasta)

Boiled meat balls (*German*)
Chelo kebab (*Persian*)
Chicken shami kebabs (*Indian*)
Chicken with potatoes
  (*Lebanese*)
Cutlets stuffed with rice
  (*Czechoslovakian*)
Escalopes with mustard sauce
  (*German*)
Khoresh (*Persian*)
Kofta curry (*Pakistani*)
Malaysian mince (*Malaysian*)
Meat balls (*Danish*)
Meat balls (*Russian*)
Meat balls (*Italian*)
Meat balls in sweet and sour
  sauce (*Chinese*)

Meat cakes (*Norwegian*)
Meat in cabbage leaves (*Polish*)
Meat sausage (*Rumanian*)
Minced chicken cutlets (*Polish*)
Minced meat curry (*Indian*)
Moussaka (*Greek*)
Mutton cakes (*Maharashtrian*)
Mutton kofta (*Armenian*)
Rissoles stuffed with mushrooms
  (*Polish*)
Shami kebabs (*Pakistani*)
Steak tartare (*Danish*)
Stuffed aubergines (*Lebanese*)
Stuffed egg roll (*Chinese*)
Stuffed green peppers (*Indian*)
Stuffed meat balls (*Persian*)

ALL ABOUT MINCE

Very little has been written on this subject and it is commonly thought of as a means of using up left-overs.

Contrary to this view in my own house I use a lot of minced meat, but *fresh, raw meat only.*

Minced beef, veal, pork or a combination of the three, mutton and even chicken can be used for a variety of main dishes as well as for various fillings and stuffings for vine or cabbage leaves, aubergines, marrows, green peppers and other kinds of vegetables. It can be used for different types of pasta or pastry, boiled, steamed or baked.

The raw, minced meat made up into cutlets, balls, steaks, sausages and so on, can be treated like any other kind of meat—fried, boiled or roasted and served with various sauces and gravies. I offer my guests a mock steak Rossini with a slice of pâté de foie gras, mushrooms (truffles would be too expensive) and Madeira sauce, which is always very popular.

For those who like curry, what could be nicer for a Sunday lunch than a 'kofta curry' made with little minced meat balls and served with boiled rice and the usual accompaniments? The same meat balls can be made smaller, skewered on sticks and offered with drinks. Similarly there are the Chinese sweet-and-sour meat balls which can also form the basis for a main dish.

The great advantage of these dishes is that they can be prepared in advance and, most important point for a housewife on a limited budget, minced meat is *inexpensive* and there is *no waste.*

I have collected a great many minced meat recipes from all over the world and, having tried them very successfully, I pass them on to my readers, hoping that they will enjoy them as much as my guests and I do.

Boiled meat balls: Königsberger Klops
(*German*)

½ lb. minced beef
¼ lb. minced pork
2 oz. kidney fat (rendered)
salt
pepper
nutmeg
½ onion, chopped
1 thick slice of white bread,
   soaked in milk

1 egg
2 chopped anchovies
1 oz. butter
1 tablesp. flour
1 tablesp. lemon juice
1 tablesp. capers
salted water

Soak the bread in milk in a bowl and squeeze. Heat the kidney fat in a frying-pan and put in the onion. Fry lightly. Put the minced meat in a bowl and mix the onion, bread, salt, pepper, nutmeg and anchovies with it. Separate the egg yolk from the white. Beat the egg yolk and whip the white. Stir the beaten egg yolk into the meat mixture. Fold in the whipped white. Form the mixture into balls. Roll in flour and drop into a pan of salted water which has been boiled and reduced to simmering point. Cook for 20 minutes. Remove from water and keep warm.

Heat 1 oz. of butter in a frying-pan. Add the flour and stir. Gradually add about 1 cup of the stock in which the meat balls were boiled. Season with salt to taste, add lemon juice and capers. Put the meat balls in this sauce and simmer for a minute or two.

Chelo kebab
(*Persian*)

1 lb. minced mutton
4 cloves garlic
6 cardamoms
1 small stick cinnamon
1 inch fresh ginger
1 teasp. cumin seeds

6 cloves
2 teasp. vinegar
salt
3 cups rice
6 oz. butter
6 egg yolks

Pound meat into a paste. Grind the garlic with the spices and add the meat, together with the vinegar. Mix well and season with salt.

Cover and leave for 2 hours. Roll into long kebabs (6 × 1½ inches). Grill them on an open coal fire or under a grill for about 10 minutes, turning them frequently.

Wash the rice and boil it in salted water (*see* Section Seven). When it is cooked, turn it onto a hot serving dish and place the kebabs on top. Put 1 egg yolk into individual serving dishes. Pour 1 oz. melted butter over each. These are served separately, and each person should mix it with the hot rice.

Note: To simplify the serving of the rice, the melted butter and egg yolks can be mixed with the hot rice and served on the dish under the kebabs.

Chicken shami kebabs
(*Indian*)

1 medium-sized chicken	2 green chillies
1 large onion	½ teasp. cumin seeds
4 cloves garlic	½ teasp. coriander seeds
1 inch fresh ginger	salt

Mince the chicken flesh. Grind the onion, garlic, ginger and spices and mix with water to a paste. Mix with chicken and season with salt. Form mixture into small balls. Put the balls on a skewer and fry in hot fat or grill them.

Note: Suitable for serving on toothpicks as savouries.

Chicken with potatoes: Mahmoosah
(*Lebanese*)

1 medium-sized chicken	1 tablesp. chopped, fresh
1 large onion, chopped	coriander leaves
2 green chillies, chopped	2 eggs
salt	oil for frying
4 medium-sized potatoes	

Mince the chicken flesh. Heat the oil in a frying-pan and sauté the chopped onion lightly, add the chicken, chillies and salt and fry for a few minutes. Add the potatoes which have been peeled and cubed. Continue frying until the potatoes are cooked (adding more oil if necessary). When cooked add coriander leaves, stir in the beaten eggs and fry until the eggs are set.

Cutlets stuffed with rice
(*Czechoslovakian*)

½ lb. minced beef or veal	pepper
½ lb. minced pork	5–6 tablesp. cooked rice
½ small onion, chopped	paprika
1 white roll or 1 slice of white bread	dried breadcrumbs
	butter or cooking fat for frying
1 egg yolk	milk or water
salt	

Heat the butter in a frying-pan and sauté lightly the chopped onion. Mix in a bowl with the minced meat. Cut off crust from bread and soak in milk or water. Squeeze and add to meat mixture. Stir in egg yolk and season with salt and pepper. Gradually add 4 tablespoons cold water and stir until mixture is well blended. Knead mixture on a floured board, then form into cutlets. Add paprika to the cooked rice and put a tablespoon of rice on each cutlet. Cover with another cutlet, press edges well down and flatten out. Coat stuffed cutlets with breadcrumbs and fry in hot fat until brown on both sides and the meat has cooked through (about 10 minutes). Brown the cutlets quickly to start with, then reduce temperature for the rest of the cooking time.

Escalopes with mustard sauce: Eskalopes mit Senfsauce
(*German*)

1 lb. beef, minced	½ teacup water
2 oz. suet or pork fat, minced	1 tablesp. French mustard
1 egg	2 tablesp. sour cream
salt	fat for frying
pepper	water or stock
2 tablesp. dried breadcrumbs	

Mix minced meat and fat together and add beaten egg and bread-crumbs. Season with salt and pepper and stir in water. Mix well, and form mixture into small escalopes. Heat some fat in a frying-pan and fry escalopes. Remove from pan and place on a serving dish. Blend mustard with cream and a little water or stock and pour into pan. Bring to boil and pour over escalopes.

Khoresh
(Persian)

1 lb. minced lamb or mutton	½ teasp. cinnamon
2 oz. oil or vegetable fat	salt
1 large onion, chopped	pepper
1 oz. lentils (soaked)	1 teasp. lemon juice
1 lb. sliced tomatoes	3 potatoes

Heat half fat in frying-pan and sauté lightly the chopped onion. Add minced meat and fry, stirring until meat is browned. Add lentils and tomatoes. Season with salt, pepper and cinnamon. Cover pan and simmer until lentils are cooked. Add a little hot water if necessary.

In another saucepan, heat the rest of the fat and fry peeled and cubed potatoes until they are golden brown. Add them to the meat, stir in lemon juice and cook for 20 minutes or until potatoes are cooked. Serve with rice.

Kofta curry
(Pakistani)

1 lb. minced beef or mutton	*For masala:*
4 cloves garlic	1 dessertsp. coriander powder
1 egg	1 teasp. turmeric powder
salt	½ teasp. cumin seed powder
¼ teasp. coriander powder	½ teasp. red chilli powder
a few fresh coriander leaves, chopped (if available)	½ teasp. cardamom powder
1 large onion, grated	salt
1½ inch fresh ginger, chopped	1 tablesp. tomato purée
water or coconut milk	ghee or oil for frying

Mix minced meat, crushed garlic, coriander powder, ginger and coriander leaves together and stir in the beaten egg. Form mixture into small balls. Heat the ghee or oil in a frying-pan and fry the balls in this. Remove balls from pan and set on one side. Fry the grated onion, cloves, ginger and masala ingredients. After a few minutes add tomato purée and salt to taste. Add sufficient hot water or coconut milk to form a thick gravy, bring to boil and return the fried meat balls to the pan. Season with more salt if required. Cover the pan and simmer until meat is cooked (about 30 minutes).

Serve with boiled rice (*see* Section Seven).

Note: Some cooks do not fry the meat balls before adding them to the sauce. In this case you should drop them carefully, one by one, into the simmering masala and continue as directed above. These balls make a delicious cocktail dish. Make balls very small, cook as directed and serve on a hot dish with the gravy with a toothpick stuck in each ball.

Malaysian mince
(*Malaysian*)

1½ lb. stewing beef
3 large onions, sliced
2 inches freshly chopped ginger
1 coconut

salt
3 green chillies, ground
juice of 1 lemon
oil for frying

Cut meat into several pieces, cover with water in a saucepan and boil until tender. Remove from pan and cool. Mince. Grate the coconut and lightly roast the flakes in a dry frying-pan. Remove from pan. Heat some oil in the pan and lightly sauté the onion. Put minced meat in a bowl with the fried coconut and onion. Add the chillies, salt and lemon juice. Heat some oil in a pan and put the mixture in. Warm on a low heat, stirring all the time.

Serve with rice.

Meat balls
(*Danish*)

1½ lb. equal amounts veal and
    pork, minced together
1 tablesp. flour
½ cup milk
2 teasp. grated onion

2 teasp. salt
pepper
1 egg yolk
1 teasp. cream
fat for frying

Put meat in a bowl and make a hollow in mixture. Fill it with flour blended with milk. Add the onion and egg yolk and season with salt and pepper. Add cream and mix all ingredients well together. Heat some fat in a pan and drop tablespoons of the mixture into it. Fry till brown on both sides.

Meat balls: Bitochki
(*Russian*)

½ lb. minced beef
½ lb. minced veal
2 tablesp. rendered kidney fat
1 teasp. salt
1-2 tablesp. chopped onion

1 slice white bread, soaked in
    milk
pepper
8 oz. mushrooms
1 cup sour cream

Heat the kidney fat in a frying-pan and sauté the onion. Mix this in a bowl with the meat. Add the bread, which has been squeezed, salt and pepper. Knead well. Form into small balls and roll in flour. Heat fat in pan and fry the balls. When cooked, remove them from the pan. Add a little water to the pan. Scrape up the juices. Return the meat balls to the pan and simmer until meat is cooked.

In a separate pan, sauté the sliced mushrooms. When cooked, add the sour cream. Pour the sauce into the pan with the meat balls. Bring to the boil and simmer for a few minutes.

Meat balls: Polpette
(*Italian*)

1 lb. equal amounts beef and veal, minced together	pepper
1 clove garlic	nutmeg
1 slice white bread, soaked in milk	1 beaten egg
	2 teasp. chopped parsley
salt	½ teasp. lemon rind, grated
	oil for frying

Put meat in a bowl with crushed garlic, bread (squeezed) and beaten egg. Season with salt and pepper and add chopped parsley, nutmeg and lemon rind. Mix well and form into small cakes.

Heat the oil in a frying-pan and fry the meat cakes slowly for about 3–4 minutes on each side.

Meat balls in sweet and sour sauce
(*Chinese*)

For the meat balls:	*For the sauce:*
1 lb. minced pork	2 tablesp. oil
1 tablesp. wine or sherry	2 green peppers, cut into strips
1 tablesp. chopped leek	2 slices pineapple, cubed
2 tablesp. soya sauce	4 tablesp. sugar
½ teasp. salt	4 tablesp. vinegar
½ teasp. Chinese pepper	3 tablesp. soya sauce
2 teasp. chopped fresh ginger	1 tablesp. wine
1 tablesp. cornflour	1 tablesp. cornflour
oil for deep frying	1 cup water

To prepare meat balls: Mix all ingredients together and form into balls. (More cornflour can be used if required to make the balls keep their shape.) Heat oil in a deep frying-pan and fry balls until brown. Remove from pan when cooked and put on a serving dish. Keep hot.

To prepare sauce: Heat 2 tablespoons oil in a small saucepan and lightly fry the green peppers and the pineapple. In a bowl mix the sugar, vinegar, soya sauce and wine together and add this to the mixture in the saucepan. Blend cornflour and water and add it to the sauce in the pan. Bring to the boil and when the sauce has thickened pour it over the meat balls.

Meat cakes
(*Norwegian*)

½ lb. minced beef	½ cup milk
½ lb. minced belly pork	black pepper
1 teasp. salt	fat for frying
a pinch ginger	

Mix all ingredients in a bowl. Form mixture into six cakes. Heat oil in a pan and fry cakes in the hot fat on both sides. Allow cakes to fry for about 7 minutes on each side.

Serve with cabbage.

Meat in cabbage leaves: Golabki
(*Polish*)

1 large cabbage	12 oz. minced pork
4 oz. rice	salt, pepper
1 oz. lard	1 cup sour cream
½ chopped onion	1 teasp. flour

Having first removed the stalk from the end of the cabbage, parboil it in salted water. When ready plunge into cold water for a minute. Remove the required number of leaves from the cabbage, keeping them whole, though cutting away any tough stalk. (The leaves can be removed from the cabbage without cooking it, but this is difficult when the cabbage is a firm one.)

Half-cook the rice in a large amount of salted water. Drain. Heat some lard in a frying-pan and fry the chopped onion. In a bowl mix these with the minced meat, salt and pepper. Place a little of this mixture on each cabbage leaf, fold the sides of the leaf over, roll up in a parcel and press gently between the palms of the hands to seal the edges.

Line a shallow pan with some of the discarded cabbage leaves and place the stuffed leaves side by side. Arrange in two or three layers, depending on the number you do. Cover with boiling water or stock, then cover with more cabbage leaves and put in a slow oven 300° F., Gas reg. 2, for about 1½ hours. Remove the leaves from the top and finish cooking uncovered. This should be for about another 30 minutes. Increase the temperature during this time to 350° F., Gas reg. 4. Remove the stuffed leaves from the pan and place on a hot serving dish. In a small saucepan blend the flour with the cream and add a little of the stock in which the stuffed leaves were cooked. Simmer for a few minutes and pour over the stuffed leaves on the serving dish.

Meat sausage: Carnati
(*Rumanian*)

1 lb. equal amounts minced beef and pork	1 teasp. paprika
1 clove garlic	pinch marjoram
1 teasp. salt	fat for roasting

Mix minced meat, salt, paprika and marjoram together. Knead well and form into a sausage. Heat fat in a roasting pan and put in sausage. Bake in a pre-heated oven 425° F., Gas reg. 7, until brown and well cooked (about 40 minutes). Baste from time to time. Remove from the tin to a serving dish. Slice and serve.

Minced chicken cutlets: Kotleciki z kury
(*Polish*)

1 chicken, about 3 lb. in weight	2 egg yolks
1 oz. bread rolls, or 1 slice white bread	dried breadcrumbs
¼ pint cream or top of milk	butter for frying
1 oz. butter	salt

Skin and bone the chicken. Mince the meat two or three times. Cream butter with the egg yolks and add this to the minced meat, season with salt. Soak the bread roll or slice in milk, squeeze out and mix with the minced chicken. Form mixture into small cutlets and coat them with breadcrumbs. Heat some butter in a frying-pan and put the cutlets

into it. Fry on both sides until golden brown in colour and cooked
through.

Serve with cauliflower, carrots, green peas or lettuce.

Minced meat curry: Kheema
(*Indian*)

1 lb. minced beef or mutton	4 tablesp. oil or ghee
2 medium-sized onions	½ teasp. ground cumin seeds
2 cloves garlic	3 medium-sized tomatoes or
2 teasp. ground coriander	1 tablesp. tomato purée
1 teasp. ground turmeric	salt
½ teasp. ground chillies	

Chop the onion and pound the garlic. Heat the fat in a frying-pan and
lightly fry the onion and garlic for 2–3 minutes. Add the spices and
continue frying for a few minutes. Add the chopped tomatoes or
tomato purée. Mix well and fry for a few minutes longer, stirring all
the time. Add the minced meat, and salt to taste. Cook slowly until
meat is cooked through and almost dry.

Note: To simplify the curry you may use 1 tablespoon curry powder
instead of the mixed spices.

Moussaka
(*Greek*)

4 medium-sized aubergines	⅓ cup wine
1 lb. minced beef	1 tablesp. chopped parsley
1 medium-sized onion	salt
oil for frying	cinnamon
1 clove garlic	1 oz. butter
5 medium-sized tomatoes or	1 oz. flour
3 tablesp. tomato purée	½ pint milk
grated Parmesan cheese	1 egg yolk
a pinch of nutmeg	

Slice the aubergines, sprinkle with salt and leave for 30 minutes.
Drain and rinse in cold water. Dry on a kitchen towel.

Heat the oil in a frying-pan. Fry the aubergines. Remove from the
pan. Heat more oil in the pan and sauté the onion, add garlic and
minced meat and fry until meat changes colour. Add the chopped
tomatoes or tomato purée, wine, parsley and cinnamon. Season with
salt. Cover the pan and simmer on a slow heat for 30 minutes.

In a saucepan melt the butter, add the flour and mix together.
Gradually add the milk, stirring all the time. When the sauce has

thickened, remove from the heat and add the egg yolk and nutmeg. Mix well.

Butter an ovenproof dish and line with aubergine slices. Put a layer of meat next and cover with a little sauce. Continue adding a layer of aubergines and a layer of meat (finishing with a layer of aubergine) until the dish is almost full. Pour the sauce over the top, sprinkle liberally with grated Parmesan cheese and cook in a hot oven (400° F., Gas reg. 6) for 30–40 minutes.

Mutton cakes: Niwala
(*Maharashtrian*)

8 oz. minced mutton
8 oz. potatoes
4 oz. cloves
1 stick cinnamon
¼ teasp. red chilli powder
oil or ghee for frying
3 cloves garlic
1 inch fresh ginger, chopped
1 teasp. salt
2 green chillies, chopped

1 small onion, chopped
1 tablesp. coriander leaves, chopped very finely
2 teasp. mint leaves, chopped very finely
1 teasp. lemon juice
1–2 eggs
1 cup water
flour for coating

Peel the potatoes and put them through a mincer. Mix them with the meat and add the cloves, cinnamon, chilli powder, ginger, finely chopped garlic and salt. Put the mixture in a saucepan. Add the onion and green chillies. Cover with water and simmer until the water has evaporated. Add the coriander and mint leaves and mix well. Add the lemon juice. Allow mixture to cool. Divide the mixture into eight and shape into cakes. Flatten them a little and dip into the beaten eggs, then into the flour.

Heat the oil or ghee in a frying-pan and fry the meat cakes on both sides until brown.

Mutton kofta
(*Armenian*)

1½ lb. minced mutton
2 tablesp. oil or ghee
1 stalk celery, chopped
1 cup curd
1 tablesp. red pepper powder
2 teasp. cumin seed powder
salt

2 tablesp. fresh coriander leaves, chopped
1 tablesp. fresh mint leaves, chopped
3 eggs
water

Heat the oil or ghee in a frying-pan and fry the meat. Add the celery and a little water. Cover and simmer until meat is quite tender and the water has evaporated. Remove from the heat and cool. Add the curd, red pepper and cumin seed powder. Season with salt. Add coriander and mint leaves and one egg. Mix well and shape into a thick roll on a floured board. Place the roll in a greased baking tin and coat the top of the roll with beaten egg. Put in a pre-heated oven (425° F., Gas reg. 7) and cook for about 1 hour, or until meat is cooked and a dark crust has formed on the top. Baste occasionally.

Rissoles stuffed with mushrooms:
Klopsiki z nadzieniem z grzybow
(*Polish*)

1 lb. minced veal	1 oz. dried mushrooms, soaked in
1 bread roll or 2 slices white	water
bread weighing in all 1½ oz.	1 oz. butter
1 egg	1 tablesp. chopped onion
salt	1 teasp. flour
pepper	½ cup sour cream
3–4 tablesp. water	chopped parsley
½ cup milk, or milk and water	fat for frying

Soak the bread roll or bread slices in milk, or milk and water, and squeeze. Mix half the bread with the minced meat. Add the egg, salt and pepper and gradually stir in the water. When ingredients are thoroughly blended, divide into 6–8 portions.

Put the mushrooms and their water in a small saucepan and cook until tender. Add more water, if necessary. Strain, but keep the liquid.

Heat butter in frying-pan and put in onion. Sauté lightly.

Cream ½ oz. butter and add the rest of the bread, mushrooms, onion, salt and pepper and mix all together.

Flatten each portion of meat and place a little of the mushroom filling in the centre of each. Form oblong rissoles and roll in flour. Heat some fat in a frying-pan and brown on all sides. Transfer to another saucepan in which the liquid from the mushrooms has been placed. Put on a low heat, cover and simmer for 20–30 minutes. (Add a little more water if required.) Take out rissoles and place on a hot serving dish. Keep warm.

Blend flour with the sour cream and add this to the juices in the

H

frying-pan in which the rissoles have been browned. Bring to the boil and cook for a few minutes. Pour the gravy over the rissoles, sprinkle with chopped parsley and serve with potatoes, barley or dumplings.

Shami kebabs
(*Pakistani*)

1 lb. minced beef or mutton	*For the filling:*
1 large onion, minced	1 onion, chopped or minced
3 oz. lentils (dhal)	2 oz. chopped sultanas
4 cloves	½ teasp. chilli powder
4 cardamoms	salt
10 peppercorns	
1 stick cinnamon	
salt	
1 egg	
¾ cup water	
ghee or oil for frying	

Mix meat and onion and put in a saucepan with water. Add lentils (which have been washed and soaked in water), cloves, cardamoms, peppercorns, cinnamon. Cover the pan and simmer on a low heat until meat and lentils are cooked and the water has been absorbed. Remove mixture from the pan and pound to a thick paste in a bowl. Blend in beaten egg and season with salt. Form the meat mixture into small balls and stuff each ball with a little of the onion filling. To do this dip your hands in water, put a little of the filling on the meat and close your hand round it to form a small ball. Heat oil or ghee in a frying-pan and drop in meat balls. Fry in hot fat until well browned and cooked through.

To prepare filling: Mix the onion with the sultanas and chilli powder and season with salt.

Steak tartare
(*Danish*)

1 lb. minced lean beef	freshly ground black pepper
1 teasp. salt	4 egg yolks

Mix raw meat with salt and pepper. Shape into four round cakes. Make a dent in the centre of each and drop in a raw egg yolk.

Serve with minced onion, capers and anchovy fillets.

Stuffed aubergines: Dolma
(*Lebanese*)

6 medium-sized aubergines
2 tablesp. cooking fat
1 large onion, chopped
1 lb. minced beef or mutton
salt
pepper
6 oz. minced beef

1 tablesp. chopped parsley
¼ teasp. cinnamon
2 oz. rice
2½ cups water
2 tablesp. lemon juice
3 dried mushrooms, soaked in water

Carefully cut off the tops of the aubergines, and put them on one side. Remove the pulp, sprinkle the insides with salt, leave for 1 hour, rinse with cold water and dry.

Boil rice in 1 cup water and drain.

Heat the fat and lightly fry the chopped onion. Add the meat and brown, add the rice, mint, parsley and cinnamon. Season with salt and pepper.

Fill the aubergines with this mixture and place the tops back on. Secure with toothpicks. Arrange in a saucepan, add 1½ cups hot water and lemon juice. Cover, and cook until the aubergines are done.

Stuffed egg roll
(*Chinese*)

3 eggs
¼ teasp. salt
3 teasp. cornflour
2 teasp. water
oil for deep frying
6 oz. minced beef

1 tablesp. soya sauce
1 tablesp. sherry or wine
½ teasp. minced fresh ginger
1 teasp. chopped leek
3 dried mushrooms, soaked in water

Beat the eggs. Add the salt. Heat 1 tablespoon oil in a 7-inch frying-pan and pour in half the egg mixture. Spread like a pancake and fry on both sides. Repeat with rest of egg.

Mix the meat with soya sauce, sherry, ginger, leek, mushrooms (chopped) and 1 teaspoon cornflour. Blend well and spread mixture on each pancake. Roll up. Seal the pancakes with a mixture of 2 teaspoons of cornflour mixed with 2 teaspoons of water. Heat some fat in a deep frying-pan. Fry rolls. Drain, and cut each diagonally into several slices.

Stuffed green peppers: Bhari mirch
(*Indian*)

6 large green peppers	1 teasp. garam masala
2 tablesp. ghee or oil	a pinch cinnamon
1 large onion, chopped	½ teasp. chilli powder
3 cloves garlic	1 tablesp. chopped fresh coriander
2 teasp. turmeric powder	leaves (if available)
1 teasp. cumin seed powder	1 lb. minced mutton or beef
2 teasp. coriander powder	salt to taste
1 cup water	

Cut off the tops of the green peppers and carefully remove the seeds and white pith.

Heat the oil in a frying-pan and lightly fry the onion, add the spices and minced meat and continue frying until the meat is well browned. Season with salt and add coriander leaves. Add hot water. Cover pan and cook until water has been absorbed, but meat not dry. Cool slightly.

Stuff prepared peppers with the meat mixture, place in a large saucepan with a little water, cover and simmer until the peppers are cooked.

Stuffed meat balls: Koofteh Irani
(*Persian*)

For meat balls:	*For stuffing:*
1½ lb. minced beef or mutton	2 oz. currants
12 oz. yellow lentils	4 oz. chopped walnuts
1 egg	1 large onion, chopped
2 oz. rice	1 oz. butter
2 teasp. turmeric powder	4 hard-boiled eggs
salt	
pepper	
fat for frying	
water	

To prepare meat balls: Boil lentils in water until soft. Drain. Mix meat and lentils and pound until soft and well blended. Cook rice and add to meat and lentil mixture. Season with salt and pepper and add turmeric powder. Mix thoroughly. Divide into four portions. Flatten each portion to a size big enough to place one hard-boiled egg in the centre and surround it with the currant and walnut mixture. Shape meat into large balls. Heat fat in a pan large enough to hold all meat balls and carefully place them in the hot fat. Fry on all sides and when browned, add boiling water. Be careful not to pour the water directly over the meat. Cook uncovered for 30 minutes. Cover the pan and simmer for 1 hour.

To prepare stuffing: Heat 1 oz. butter in a frying-pan. Fry currants for 1 minute, remove from pan and place in a bowl. Sauté the onion in the pan and put in the bowl. Add chopped walnuts and mix well together.

See Section Seven for further minced meat dishes.

SECTION SEVEN

Further Dishes made with Flour and other Cereal, and Dishes made with Rice

Dishes made with flour and other cereal

Bliny (*Russian*)
Calzone (*Italian*)
Chicken puffs (*Iraqi*)
Dough crumbs (*Hungarian*)
Dough squares with mushrooms
(*Polish*)
Dumplings:
  Bread (*Slovakian*)
  Breadcrumb (*Austrian*)
  Cheese (*Polish*)
  Matzo (*Israeli*)
  Potato doughnuts
    (*Czechoslovakian*)
  Potato (*Polish*)
  Raw potato (*Polish*)
  Stuffed potato (*Polish*)
  Rice (*Indian*)
  Semolina (*Yugoslav*)
Fried cheese patties (*Italian*)
Fried noodles with vegetables
(*Chinese*)
Gnocchi Roman style (*Italian*)

Gnocchi with cheese (*Yugoslav*)
Ham roll (*Yugoslav*)
Indian bread:
  Chupatties
  Parathas
  Puries
Macaroni (*Slovenian*)
Maize fritters (*Indian*)
Maize meal (*Serbian*)
Meat pasty (*Russian*)
Mutton patties (*Maharashtrian*)
Noodles (*Chinese*)
Pancakes with lobster (*French*)
Pancakes stuffed with mush-
  rooms (*Polish*)
Pasta al forno alla Romana
  (*Italian*)
Pasta with cream (*Italian*)
Patties with buckwheat flour
  (*Ukrainian*)
Potato fritters (*Parsee*)
Ravioli (*Chinese*)

Ravioli (*Lithuanian*)   Spaghetti with peas (*Italian*)
Ravioli (*Ukrainian*)   Steamed dumplings (*Tibetan*)
Ravioli with mushrooms (*Polish*)   Stuffed pancakes (*Chinese*)

Dishes made with rice

Chinese method of cooking rice   Mutton pilau with buriani
Indian method of cooking rice   (*Arabian*)
Aubergine pilau (*Indian*)   Rice with cherries (*Persian*)
Bagdad pilau (*Iraqi*)   Rice with chicken (*Indian*)
Chicken pilau (*Indian*)   Risotto Milanese (*Italian*)
Dubrovnik rice (*Dalmation*)   Spanish rice (*Spanish*)
Fried rice (*Chinese*)   White rice (*Afghanistan*)
Moulmein rice (*Burmese*)

PASTA

In Italy any pasta dish is served as an entrée only, but most of these dishes can make a substantial meal on their own. I have tried to give the exact recipes with the appropriate ingredients, which in Italian dishes consist largely of cheese, such as Mozzarella, Ricotta, Parmesan and Gruyère. Some of these may not always be available so I have used cream cheese instead of Ricotta, and substituted for Mozzarella any mild English cheese.

The idea would not be approved by an Italian cook, but the use of Cheddar or Gruyère only, although not producing an orthodox Italian dish, has been proved to give excellent results.

DISHES MADE WITH FLOUR
AND OTHER CEREAL

Bliny
(*Russian*)

4 oz. buckwheat flour	¼ pint milk (approx.)
2 oz. flour	2 egg yolks
½ teasp. salt	1 egg white
½ oz. yeast	fat for frying
½ teasp. sugar	

Sift the flour and salt into a bowl and make a hollow in the centre.
Cream the yeast with sugar and add a little of the lukewarm milk.
Pour the yeast mixture into the flour and stir enough of the flour into
the yeast to make a thick sponge. Cover the bowl with a cloth and let
the sponge rise in a warm place for about 30 minutes. Beat the egg
yolks with the rest of the warmed milk and gradually add this to the
sponge, beating well. The mixture should be of consistency of a
pancake batter. If necessary add more warmed milk. Cover the bowl
and let it stand again in a warm place for about 1 hour, or until risen.
Fold in the stiffly beaten egg white. Heat the fat in a small frying-pan
(about 5 inches in diameter) or pour 1 tablespoon of the batter into a
bigger frying-pan and spread it thinly and evenly. Fry quickly on both
sides and remove to a hot dish.

Serve the blinis with red or black caviar, melted butter and sour
cream.

Note: Buckwheat flour is not always available and the blinis made
with plain flour I have found equally delicious.

Calzone
(*Italian*)

8 oz. flour	4 oz. Mozzarella cheese
¼ teasp. salt	3 oz. ham
½ oz. yeast	salt
½ cup water	pepper
1 tablesp. oil	oil for cooking

Sieve the flour and salt into a bowl and add the yeast which has been diluted with the water, slightly warmed. Mix well and add the oil. Knead into a dough, cover and leave in a warm place to rise. Leave until it has doubled its bulk. Roll out thinly and cut into rounds about 4 inches in diameter. Brush each circle with oil and place a thin slice of cheese and a little ham (which has already been chopped) on the circles. Sprinkle with salt and pepper. Fold in half and seal the edges well. Grease a baking tin with oil and place the calzone on it. Brush with oil and cook in a pre-heated oven at 450° F., Gas reg. 8, for 20 minutes. Serve hot.

Chicken puffs
(*Iraqi*)

For the pastry:	For the filling:
6 oz. flour	2 breasts of chicken, or the meat
3 tablesp. oil	of half a chicken (minced)
pinch salt	1 small onion, chopped
water	1 teasp. turmeric powder
	salt
	pepper
	1 dessertsp. chopped coriander
	leaves
	1 egg
	2 tablesp. oil

To prepare the pastry: Put the flour in a bowl, make a hollow in the centre and pour in the oil and salt and enough cold water to make soft, pliable dough. Knead until dough feels like velvet, roll out thinly and cut into rounds about 2 inches in diameter. Place a teaspoon of the mixture on each round, fold it over, sealing the edges firmly. Heat fat in a deep frying-pan and fry the puffs until golden in colour. Drain on kitchen paper and serve.

To prepare the filling: Heat the oil in a frying-pan and sauté the onion lightly. Add the minced chicken, salt, pepper, turmeric powder and coriander leaves. Stir until the chicken changes colour and is cooked. Add the beaten egg and stir for another minute, or until the egg is set.

Dough crumbs: Tarhonya
(*Hungarian*)

12 oz. flour	1 teasp. salt
3 eggs	

Sift the flour and salt into a bowl and make a well in the centre. Pour the slightly beaten eggs in and mix together gradually, adding a little more flour if necessary to make a firm dough. Knead on a floured board until elastic and perfectly smooth. Divide into a few pieces and allow to dry. Chop the dough with a big knife or grate it on a coarse grater and spread the dough on a floured cloth to dry again. Put the crumbs into a sieve and let the surplus flour pass through. Place the crumbs on a tray and dry in a cool oven. These will then keep in a jar for any length of time. When you wish to use them, cook in salted boiling water for about 15 minutes. Serve with chicken or meat broth or as an accompaniment to meats with a rich gravy.

Dough squares with mushrooms: Lazanki z Grzybami
(Polish)

12 oz. flour	pepper
2–3 eggs	1 oz. butter
salt	1 cup cream
1 lb. mushrooms, sliced	2 egg yolks
1 small onion, chopped	grated cheese

Sift the flour and salt into a bowl. Add the eggs and, if necessary, water. Mix into a stiff dough. Divide the dough into two and roll each half on a floured board. Leave on the board, or on a floured cloth for 30 minutes to dry. Cut the dough into wide strips and put them on top of one another, sprinkling flour between each layer to prevent the pieces from sticking to one another. Cut the stacked strips into ½-inch wide pieces and cut again to form tiny squares. Boil these squares in salted water for 5 minutes. Drain.

Heat the butter in a frying-pan and sauté the onion till golden in colour, add the mushrooms, season with salt and pepper and stir for a few minutes.

Butter an ovenproof dish and put the dough squares in it. Add the mushroom mixture. Blend the egg yolks with the cream and pour over it. Sprinkle with grated cheese and cook in a hot oven for 30 minutes, or until the cheese has melted and the top is brown.

Bread dumplings: Jemne knedliki
(Slovakian)

10 oz. stale breakfast rolls	2 eggs
1 cup milk	salt
2 oz. butter	butter for frying

Slice 4 oz. of the rolls. Put them in a bowl, cover with milk and leave to soak. When they are quite soft, mash them well with a fork or pass them through a sieve. Cut up the rest of the rolls into small cubes. Heat the butter in a pan, fry the bread cubes until golden in colour. Mix the cubes with the mashed rolls. Separate the yolks and the whites of the 2 eggs. Cream 2 oz. butter and add the egg yolks one by one. Add this to the bread mixture. Whisk the egg whites until quite stiff and fold this into the mixture. Season with salt. Roll the mixture into a sausage on a floured board, and place on a sheet of paper which has been liberally greased. Roll up the paper and secure the edges. Put the roll on a piece of muslin or a napkin and place in a large pan of boiling, salt water. The end of the cloth should be suspended over the edges of the pan for easy removal. Cover the pan and simmer gently for 45 minutes to 1 hour. Remove the cloth and the paper carefully. Cut the roll into thick slices and serve with meat and thick gravy.

Breadcrumb dumplings: Broselknodel
(*Austrian*)

1 cup dried breadcrumbs	½ oz. butter
1 cup scalded milk	1 oz. flour
2 eggs	salt

Put the breadcrumbs into a bowl and pour the scalded milk over them. Mix well and season with salt. Separate the egg yolks and the whites. Mix the butter and the egg yolks together and add to the breadcrumb mixture. Whisk the egg whites until quite stiff and fold into the mixture. Having dipped your hands in water or flour, form the mixture into small balls and place them on a floured board. Boil the dumplings in salted water until they float to the top and puff up (about 10–15 minutes).

Serve with stews and ragout.

Cheese dumplings: Leniwe pierogi
(*Polish*)

For dumplings:	For topping:
1 lb. cottage cheese	3 oz. butter
3 eggs	3 tablesp. dried breadcrumbs
½ oz. butter	
1 tablesp. dried breadcrumbs	
4 oz. flour	

To prepare the dumplings: Separate the egg yolks from the whites. Cream the butter and the yolks and mix with the cheese. Add the breadcrumbs and the flour. Mix well. Whisk the egg whites until quite stiff and fold this into the mixture. Flour a pastry board and roll the cheese dough into a long sausage. Flatten the roll slightly and cut into pieces about 1½ inches long.

Prepare a saucepan of boiling salted water and drop in the dumplings one by one. Simmer gently for about 10 minutes, remove them from the pan and drain carefully. Put them on a heated serving dish, and keep warm.

To prepare the topping: Melt half the butter in a frying-pan and fry the breadcrumbs until golden in colour. Add the rest of the butter, stir until it has melted and pour the mixture over the dumplings.

These dumplings are served as a separate dish and are suitable for a light supper.

Matzo dumplings
(*Israeli*)

1 cup matzo meal	pepper
1 egg	ground ginger (optional)
3 tablesp. melted chicken fat	water
salt	

Put the matzo meal in a bowl. Make a hollow in the centre and drop in the beaten egg mixed with the chicken fat. Mix and season with salt and pepper and add the ginger if desired. Add enough cold water to make a soft, pliable batter and leave this to stand for several hours so that the meal can absorb the liquid. Dip hands into water, then shape the batter into medium-sized balls and cook gently in salted boiling water for about 20–30 minutes.

Potato doughnuts: Bramborove Koblizky
(*Czechoslovakian*)

1 lb. potatoes	1 oz. yeast
1 oz. butter	¼ pint milk
1 egg	8 oz. flour
salt	lard for deep frying
pepper	

Peel and boil the potatoes. Mash them and place them in a bowl.

Season with salt and pepper and add the butter, egg, yeast diluted in warm milk, and flour, and knead into a firm dough. Roll out on a floured board and cut into small rounds. Form the rounds into balls and replace them on the floured board. Put them in a warm place to rise. Heat the fat in a deep pan and drop the doughnuts into the boiling fat. Reduce the heat, cover the pan and cook the doughnuts slowly. When nearly cooked, take off the lid and finish the cooking with the pan uncovered. When the doughnuts are brown remove from the pan and drain. They should be served immediately.

Note: Doughnuts can be filled with a little cooked minced meat before they are put to rise.

Potato dumplings: Kluski kartoflane
(*Polish*)

1 lb. potatoes	1 egg yolk
½ oz. butter	4 oz. flour
salt	

Peel the potatoes, boil and mash them. Add the butter while the potatoes are hot, then add a little salt and mix well. Cool a little, mix in the flour and egg yolk. Knead into a dough. Roll the potato dough into a long sausage shape on a floured board and cut it into small pieces. Form the pieces into finger-length oblongs and drop them one by one into a large saucepan of boiling salted water. Simmer for about 5 minutes or until the dumplings float to the top. Drain carefully and place on a hot, buttered dish.

Serve with meat.

Raw potato dumplings: Kluski z surowych kartofli
(*Polish*)

1 lb. potatoes	pepper
salt	1½ tablesp. flour

Grate finely the raw potatoes, place them in a muslin bag and squeeze out the juice into a bowl. Leave the juice to settle. Keep the residue. Put the raw potato into a bowl with the residue from the liquid. Season with salt and pepper and mix in the flour. Form into small balls and boil in a large quantity of boiling salted water for about 15–20 minutes, or until they float to the top.

Serve with beef or veal stews.

Stuffed potato dumplings: Pyzy
(*Polish*)

2 lb. potatoes
1 egg
salt
flour
8 oz. boiled or roasted meat (beef or veal)

1 small bread roll or 1 slice of white bread
½ chopped onion
1 oz. lard
pork fat (with crackling)

Peel, boil and mash 1 lb. potatoes. Grate finely the remaining raw potatoes and leave to drain in a sieve placed over a bowl. Mix the raw potatoes with the mashed potatoes and add the residue of liquid which has collected in the bowl from the raw potatoes. Add the egg and salt and knead the mixture into a dough on a floured board. Roll into a long sausage shape and cut into pieces about 1½ inches long.

Soak the bread in water and squeeze it out. Mince the meat and combine it with the softened bread. Heat some fat in a frying-pan. Fry the chopped onion and add this to the meat mixture. Season with salt and pepper and mix well.

Flatten the potato pieces into small rounds and stuff them with the meat mixture. Bring the edges together and seal firmly. Form the potato rounds into small dumplings about the size of a big walnut and drop them into the boiling salted water. (Try one of the dumplings first. If it is too soft and comes apart, add 2–3 tablespoons of flour to the dough.) Boil for about 5 minutes. Take them out with a spoon. Place on a hot dish.

Melt the pork fat, cut into cubes, and when the crackling is cooked and brown, pour the fat and crackling over the dumplings.

Rice dumplings
(*Indian*)

1 cup cooked rice
2 oz. besan flour (gram flour)
½ teasp. red chilli powder
½ teasp. turmeric powder
6 tablesp. oil
chopped coriander leaves
2 whole dried chillies

½ teasp. cumin seeds
½ teasp. mustard seeds
½ inch fresh ginger, ground with 2 green chillies
2 cups sour milk or yoghurt
2 cups water
salt

Put the cooked rice in a bowl and add the besan flour, chilli powder, turmeric and 3 tablespoons of oil. Mix well and add a little water to make a soft dough. Roll into oblong dumplings about 1½ inches long and set on one side.

Heat 3 tablespoons oil in a deep pan and add the whole chillies, cumin seeds, mustard seeds and the ginger mixture. Mix well and fry. Add sour milk and water. Season with salt and bring to the boil. Drop rice dumplings into the simmering sour milk mixture and simmer them for 5 minutes or until the dumplings are tender and puffed up.

Serve on a hot dish garnished with coriander leaves.

Semolina dumplings
(Yugoslav)

1 lb. curd cheese	2 oz. semolina
3 oz. butter	3 tablesp. flour
2 eggs	2 tablesp. dried breadcrumbs

Mix together the cheese, 1 oz. butter and beaten eggs. Stir in the semolina and add enough flour to enable the mixture to be formed into small balls. Prepare a saucepan of boiling salted water and drop in the dumplings one by one. Cook gently for 5–7 minutes..

Melt 1 oz. butter in a frying-pan and fry the breadcrumbs until golden in colour. Add the rest of the butter and pour this mixture over the drained dumplings which should be put on a hot dish. These dumplings make an excellent light supper dish.

Fried cheese patties: Fritelli di ricotta
(Italian)

For pasta	For filling:
8 oz. flour	1 oz. butter
½ teasp. salt	1 egg yolk
1 egg yolk	8 oz. ricotta cheese
1 teasp. olive oil	2 oz. grated Parmesan
tepid water	salt
	pepper
	nutmeg
	oil for frying

To prepare pasta: Put flour in a bowl. Add salt, egg yolk, olive oil and enough water to make a firm dough. Knead well until smooth then roll out thinly. (Divide into 2 or 3 and roll out each separately.) Cut the sheets of pasta into squares about 2 inches wide and place a little of the cheese mixture on one square and cover it with another.

Press edges firmly together. Heat oil in a frying-pan and fry patties on both sides until golden in colour. Drain and serve very hot.

To prepare filling: Cream butter and egg yolk. Add cheese, season with salt and pepper and add nutmeg. Mix well.

Fried noodles with vegetables
(*Chinese*)

For noodles:
8 oz. flour
3 eggs

For garnish:
Omelette made from 1 egg and cut into strips

For vegetable base:
3 tablesp. oil
1 clove garlic
½ onion, sliced thinly
4 oz. shredded cabbage
2 shredded carrots
4 oz. fresh bean sprouts or 1 small tin
4 oz. sliced French beans
1 inch fresh ginger, finely chopped
1 tablesp. soya sauce
1 cup hot stock or water
2 teasp. cornflour
salt
sugar

To prepare noodles: Place flour in a mound on a pastry board and make a hollow in the centre. Lightly beat the eggs and pour into the flour. Mix well and knead into a dough. Cover with a damp cloth and allow to stand for 20 minutes. Knead again. Roll out the dough very thinly. Fold loosely and cut across into very fine strips. Drop in a pan full of boiling salted water and boil for 3 minutes. Drain and rinse with cold water. Put aside.

Note: Chinese noodles can be obtained in Chinese shops. If you wish to use them, do so. Cook according to directions.

To prepare vegetable base: Heat oil in a deep frying-pan and fry chopped garlic and onion for a minute or two. Add the vegetables (except the bean sprouts) and fry for 2–3 minutes. Add the bean sprouts and continue frying for 5 minutes. Keep vegetables hot. Blend the cornflour with a little water and add to the hot stock. Add sugar, salt and ginger and stir in soya sauce. Add vegetables to this liquid and cover the pan. Cook for 3–5 minutes.

In another deep frying-pan, heat oil and fry the noodles until they are a golden colour. Remove them and mix them with the vegetables.

Place everything on a serving dish and garnish with an omelette cut into strips.

Gnocchi Roman style
(*Italian*)

1 pint milk	½ oz. butter
4–5 oz. semolina	2 beaten eggs
salt	2 oz. grated Parmesan cheese
nutmeg	

Add salt and a pinch of nutmeg to the milk and heat it in a saucepan. When it boils, gradually add the semolina, stirring all the time to prevent lumps forming. Cook until the mixture is very thick. Remove from the heat and stir in the butter and eggs. Add the cheese, mix well and spread the mixture about ½ inch thick on a flat buttered dish or tin. Leave to cool. When cold, cut rounds or squares from the mixture and arrange these, overlapping, in a shallow well-buttered dish. Sprinkle with grated cheese and melted butter and brown in a hot oven (400° F., Gas reg. 6). When the cheese has melted the gnocchi are ready to serve.

Gnocchi with cheese
(*Yugoslav*)

2 lb. potatoes	salt
10 oz. flour	8 oz. cottage cheese
3 egg yolks or	2 oz. butter
1 egg and 1 yolk	1 oz. breadcrumbs

Peel and boil the potatoes in salted water. Mash them and place in a bowl to cool. Add flour, 2 egg yolks or 1 egg and a little salt and mix well. Transfer dough onto a floured pastry board and cut into pieces. Flatten each piece to a round about 2 inches in diameter and place in the centre a teaspoonful of cottage cheese which has previously been mixed with an egg yolk and seasoned with salt. Bring edges together, seal well and roll into small dumplings. Prepare a saucepan of boiling salted water. Drop in the dumplings one by one. Reduce heat and simmer until the dumplings float to the top. Take them out and put on a hot serving dish. Melt some butter and fry the breadcrumbs for about 1 minute or until golden brown in colour. Pour the fried breadcrumbs over the gnocchi. This is suitable for a light supper dish.

Ham roll: Savijaci od sunki
(*Yugoslav*)

10 oz. flour	1 oz. butter
2 oz. lard or oil	4 egg whites
¾ cup lukewarm water (approx.)	1 oz. grated Parmesan cheese
a few drops vinegar	salt
1 lb. boiled ham	pepper

Sieve the flour into a bowl and rub 1 oz. lard or oil into it. Add enough lukewarm water and a few drops of vinegar to make a smooth, pliable dough. Knead well until the dough is quite elastic and little blisters appear on the surface. Cover with a cloth and leave for 1 hour. Spread a tablecloth on the kitchen table, sprinkle it with flour and roll out the pastry as thinly as possible. Sprinkle it with melted lard or oil as you roll it. Put your hands underneath the dough and very carefully start to stretch it. When finished it should be as thin as tissue paper. Cut the thicker edges away. Sprinkle with more melted lard or oil and leave for 45 minutes before adding the filling. Spread the filling evenly over the pastry and gently lift the cloth to roll the pastry into one thick roll. Place on a greased baking tin and bake in a pre-heated oven 375° F., Gas reg. 5, for about 30 minutes. Cut into slices. Place on a serving dish and serve hot.

To prepare filling: Either mince the ham or chop it finely and add 1 oz. melted butter. Whip the egg whites until stiff and fold into the ham mixture. Season with salt and pepper and fold in grated cheese.

Note: If preferred, ready-made strudel pastry, obtainable from most delicatessen shops, may be used for this dish.

Indian bread

Indians make Chupatties, Parathas and Puries with 'atta', a coarse flour for which wholemeal and ordinary plain flour mixed in equal proportions may be substituted. They should be cooked on the top of the stove on an iron plate and eaten at once. Indian cooks do not use a rolling-pin. They form the dough into balls and flatten them between the palms of their hands.

Chupatties

1 lb. atta	water
salt	

Mix flour and salt in a bowl and add sufficient water to make a soft dough. Cover and leave for 30 minutes. Knead well and divide into 10 balls. Roll out each ball to about 7 inches in diameter. Cook on both sides on an ungreased hot plate or in a thick frying-pan.

Parathas

1 lb. atta	salt
4 oz. ghee or butter	water

Rub the ghee or butter into the flour in a bowl. Add salt and mix with cold water to form a soft dough. Knead until it feels soft and pliable. Divide into 12 and roll out like 'Chupatties'. Brush melted butter or ghee on each piece and fold edges to centre in the form of an envelope. Roll out and repeat the process. Cook on a lightly greased griddle, brushing the edges of the parathas with ghee or butter. Turn and cook the other side until the parathas are golden brown and flaky.

Puries

8 oz. atta	1 table. ghee or butter
½ teasp. salt	oil or ghee for frying

Mix the flour with the salt in a bowl and rub in the butter or ghee. Add sufficient cold water to make a pliable dough. Shape the dough into 15–20 balls and roll them out to ¼-inch thick. Heat oil or ghee in a deep frying-pan and fry them until they are puffed up and golden in colour.

Macaroni
(*Slovenian*)

1 lb. macaroni	¼ pint tomato purée diluted with
2 oz. butter	water
2 tablesp. grated cheese	½ pint cream
salt	2 eggs
pepper	water

Break macaroni into pieces and boil in salted water until almost cooked. Drain. Grease an ovenproof dish and place half the macaroni in it. Slice the butter thinly or cut it into small pieces and scatter over the macaroni. Season with salt and pepper and sprinkle the grated cheese over it. Pour in the tomato purée and put the rest of the macaroni on top. Beat the eggs, blend with cream and cover the dish with the mixture. Pre-heat oven to 400° F., Gas reg. 6, and cook for 20–30 minutes.

Maize fritters: Makka pakora
(*Indian*)

8 oz. maize flour	water
2 teasp. flour	a few small pieces cauliflower or
½ onion, chopped	carrots and turnips mixed
3 finely chopped green chillies	(cooked)
salt	oil for deep frying

Sieve the maize flour and plain flour into a bowl. Add the onion, chillies and enough cold water to make a thick batter. Season with salt and stir in vegetables. Heat the oil in a deep pan and drop dessert-spoonfuls of the mixture into the boiling oil. Reduce the heat and fry till golden in colour. Drain and serve hot.

Maize meal: Cicvara
(*Serbian*)

This is a very popular dish in Serbia and it is customary among the Orthodox Serbians to cook the 'cicvara' at Epiphany and send it round to their friends and relations.

8 oz. maize flour	1½ oz. butter
1 teasp. salt	cottage cheese
2 pints water	

Bring the water and salt to boil in a deep pan. Add ½ oz. butter and when this has melted gradually add the maize flour. Lower the heat and simmer slowly, stirring occasionally with a wooden spoon to prevent lumps from forming. Cook for 20–25 minutes. Place on a heated dish, cover liberally with cottage cheese and pour the rest of the butter (which has been melted and is slightly brown) over the dish.

Meat pasty: Pirog s gaviadinoy
(*Russian*)

For dough:	*For filling:*
8 oz. flour	2 oz. cooking fat
pinch salt	1 small onion, chopped
½ oz. yeast	1 lb. minced beef
½ teasp. sugar	salt
5 tablesp. milk	pepper
1 egg	1 tablesp. chopped parsley
2 oz. softened butter	¼ cup stock or water
	2 hard-boiled eggs
For glazing:	
1 beaten egg	

To prepare dough: Sift the flour and salt into a bowl. Make a hollow in the centre and pour in the yeast creamed with sugar and 2 tablespoons lukewarm milk. Cover with a cloth and leave to rise in a warm place for about 20 minutes. Add rest of lukewarm milk and the beaten egg. Beat well. Knead dough and gradually add the softened butter, beating well after each addition of butter. Continue kneading the dough until it is smooth and shiny but does not stick to the hand (add more flour to prevent this, if necessary). Cover and leave in a warm place until it has doubled its bulk. Roll out the dough on a floured board into an oblong ¾-inch thick and spread the warm meat mixture over the dough, leaving a 3-inch border. Moisten the edges and roll up the dough pressing the edges tightly. Place the roll on a greased baking tin and leave in a warm place for 30 minutes. Make 2–3 slits on the top to allow the steam to escape. Brush with beaten egg. Bake in a pre-heated oven at 400° F., Gas reg. 6, for 15 minutes. Reduce heat to 350° F., Gas reg. 4, and bake for a further 20–30 minutes.

To prepare filling: Heat fat in pan and sauté lightly the chopped onion. Add minced meat and stir it until it is brown, then add the seasoning, parsley and stock or water. Continue cooking until the meat is done and liquid absorbed. Remove from heat and cool a little, but do not allow to go cold. Add the hard-boiled eggs.

Mutton patties: Kheema samosas
(*Maharashtrian*)

8 oz. flour	*For the filling:*
1 dessertsp. oil	1 dessertsp. oil
salt	6 oz. minced mutton
water	4 oz. cooked green peas
oil for deep frying	3 green chillies, chopped
	2 spring onions, chopped
	1 tablesp. fresh chopped coriander leaves
	1 teasp. turmeric powder
	salt to taste

Add salt, oil and enough water to the flour to form a stiff dough. Knead well and roll out very thinly. Cut into rounds about 2 inches in diameter. Place a teaspoon of the meat mixture on each round and cover with another round. Press edges firmly. Heat the oil in a deep pan and when it boils drop in the rounds a few at a time. Cook on a slow heat until golden brown. Drain and serve hot.

To prepare the filling: Heat the oil in a saucepan, add the minced meat and stir for a while. Add the peas, chillies, chopped onion, turmeric powder and salt. Simmer slowly until mixture is quite dry. Remove from heat and add chopped coriander leaves. Mix well.

Noodles: Mah mee
(*Chinese*)

1 lb. Chinese noodles	½ lb. pork or chicken meat,
lard or oil for frying	shredded
½ medium-sized onion, sliced	1 teasp. fresh ginger, chopped
2 cloves garlic	1 tablesp. soya sauce
5 dried mushrooms, soaked in water	omelette made from 2 eggs and cut into strips

The noodles have to be boiled in water and fried in fat, so have two pans ready. Fill one with boiling water and the other with fat. Drop the noodles into the boiling water. Remove and drain well in order to get rid of any excess water. Next drop them into the boiling fat. Cook for 4–5 minutes. Take them out of the fat and put them into the boiling water again to make them soft. Put 2 tablespoons of fat in a frying-pan and heat it. Take out noodles from the water, shake well and fry in shallow fat until crisp. Put on a hot serving dish and keep warm.

Add more fat to the frying-pan and fry onion, pounded garlic, pork or chicken, ginger, mushrooms, soya sauce and 2 tablespoons of stock or water. Simmer for 7–10 minutes. Place this on top of the noodles and decorate with strips of omelette. This dish can also be garnished with pieces of crab meat, sliced raw cucumber and spring onions.

Pancakes with Lobster: Crêpes de langouste
(*French*)

	For sauce:
12 very thin pancakes	1 oz. butter
6 small lobsters (boiled)	8 oz. sliced mushrooms
½ teasp. paprika	1 large sliced tomato
salt	salt
½ pint thick, white sauce	pepper
a pinch of nutmeg	1–2 tablesp. brandy
2 teasp. tomato sauce	½ cup double cream

Mince or finely chop the boiled lobsters and season with salt and paprika. Prepare the white sauce and add a pinch of nutmeg to it. Stir in the tomato sauce and add the chopped lobsters. Fill each pancake with this mixture, roll up and fold in the ends. Place the pancakes on a fireproof dish, pour the sauce over and put in a hot oven for about 5 minutes. Serve at once.

To prepare the sauce: Heat the butter in a frying-pan and sauté the mushrooms and the tomato. When done, add seasoning and brandy. Stir in the cream and bring to the boil.

To prepare pancake batter: See below.

Pancakes stuffed with mushrooms: Nalesniki z grzybami
(*Polish*)

For pancakes:
4 oz. flour
1 egg
pinch of salt
½ pint milk and water mixed
small piece of pork fat

For coating:
1 egg
breadcrumbs
fat for frying

For filling:
12 oz. mushrooms
2 tablesp. chopped onion
1 oz. butter
1 tablesp. dried breadcrumbs
1 egg
1–2 tablesp. sour cream
salt
black pepper, freshly ground

Mix the flour and salt together; make a well in the centre and break the egg into it. Gradually stir in the flour adding half of the liquid. Beat well and add the remainder of the liquid. Leave to stand for at least 1 hour. Heat an omelette pan and grease with a piece of pork fat stuck on a fork. Pour in sufficient batter to cover the pan thinly. Cook over a medium heat until golden brown. Turn and cook the other side. Continue until all the batter has been used.

Wash and dry the mushrooms, slice them thinly. Lightly sauté the chopped onion in the melted butter for a few minutes, then add the sliced mushrooms and continue frying slowly until the mushrooms are tender. Remove from heat and add the breadcrumbs, the beaten egg and the sour cream. Season with salt and pepper. Fill the pancakes with the mixture, roll up and fold in the ends. Dip each pancake in the beaten egg, roll in breadcrumbs and fry in hot fat until golden brown.

Pasta al forno alla Romana
(*Italian*)

For pasta:
8 oz. flour
1 egg
½ teasp. salt
water
olive oil

For white sauce:
2 oz. butter
2 tablesp. flour
1 pint milk
salt
nutmeg

For meat filling:
1 lb. minced beef
1 small onion, chopped
1 clove garlic, chopped
1 lb. tinned tomatoes or 4 tablesp.
  tomato purée
salt
pepper
thyme
1 teasp. dried basil or fresh
  chopped basil
Mozzarella cheese
Parmesan cheese

To prepare pasta: Sift flour and salt on to a pastry board. Make a hollow in the centre and break the egg into it. Add a little water and mix to a fairly stiff dough. Knead it well until it feels elastic to the touch, roll it out thinly on a floured board. Cut the pasta into pieces to the shape and size of the dish in which it will be cooked. Heat a saucepan full of salted water and when the water is boiling drop the pasta pieces into it, one by one. Add a few drops of olive oil to prevent the pasta from sticking. Boil for 5 minutes. Remove from pan, rinse in cold water and drain.

To prepare meat filling: Heat 2 tablespoons oil in a pan and sauté lightly the chopped onion. Add the garlic and meat and continue frying until the meat is brown. Add the tomatoes (and liquid) or tomato purée. Season with salt and pepper and add the herbs. Cover the pan and simmer on a slow heat for about 1 hour. If meat becomes dry, add a little water or stock, but when ready the meat should not be too liquid.

To prepare the white sauce: Melt the butter in a saucepan. Add the flour and allow to cook for a few minutes. Gradually add the milk, salt and nutmeg and cook until sauce has thickened.

Grease a deep ovenproof dish or cake tin. Place one piece of the pasta on the bottom. Cover with thin layers of white sauce, slices of Mozzarella cheese and grated Parmesan cheese and cooked meat. Repeat until all has been used up. The last layer should be pasta. Cover the top layer of pasta with the remaining white sauce, sprinkle liberally with Parmesan cheese and cook in a pre-heated oven 400° F., Gas reg. 6, for 20–30 minutes.

Note: Instead of the home-made pasta, you can use bought 'lasagne'.

Pasta with cream: Rigatoni alla crema
(*Italian*)

1 lb. rigatoni	salt
1½ oz. butter	pepper
4 oz. cooked ham	10 oz. double cream
8 oz. sliced mushrooms	

Heat the butter in a pan and sauté the ham which has been cut into small pieces. Add the mushrooms and cook until they are ready. Season with salt and pepper. Cook pasta in boiling salted water and strain. Return pasta to the hot, dry pan. Add mushrooms and ham and stir in cream. Place on a hot dish and serve.

Patties with buckwheat flour: Leznie
(*Ukrainian*)

4 oz. flour	6 oz. cottage cheese
8 oz. buckwheat flour	1 egg
hot water	1 tablesp. sour cream
salt	and
lard for frying	2 cups sour cream

Put the flour in a bowl, add salt and enough boiling water to make a thick dough. Cool a little, then form into small flat rounds on a floured board. Cream the cheese and mix with the egg and 1 tablespoon of sour cream. Season with salt. Place a small mound of cheese mixture on one round of the dough and cover with another. Press edges firmly together. Heat lard in a frying-pan and fry the patties in hot fat. Fry on both sides. Serve very hot with sour cream.

Potato fritters: Bhajias
(*Parsee*)

5 large potatoes	½ teasp. cumin powder
2 eggs	1 dessertsp. vinegar
6 green chillies, chopped	1 teasp. salt or to tast
1 large onion, chopped	4 tablesp. flour
1 teasp. coriander powder	ghee or oil for frying

Peel the potatoes, boil and mash them. Cool them a little and add the beaten eggs, chillies, onion, salt and spices. Stir in the vinegar and enough flour to make a very soft dough. Sprinkle a pastry board with flour and roll the mixture into a long sausage. Take small portions of the mixture and form into balls, about the size of a walnut. Roll in flour. Heat fat in a deep frying-pan and drop the balls in. Fry quickly till golden brown and serve hot.

Ravioli: Chiao tzu
(*Chinese*)

12 oz. flour	1 tablesp. sesame oil
1 cup boiling water	2 teasp. chopped fresh ginger
8 oz. minced pork or beef	2 tablesp. soya sauce
6 oz. shredded cabbage	½ onion, chopped

Mix the flour and boiling water in a bowl to a soft dough. Cover and allow to stand for 30 minutes. Knead well and roll out very thinly on a floured board. Cut the dough into rounds about 3 inches in diameter. Put the minced meat into another bowl and add the cabbage (pressed to remove all liquid) oil, ginger, soya sauce, and onion. Mix well and place a little of this mixture in the centre of each round. Roll over and press edges firmly. Drop the ravioli into a large pan of boiling salted water and cook until they float to the top.

Ravioli: Kolduny
(*Lithuanian*)

6 oz. minced mutton (leg)	pepper
6 oz. minced fillet beef	marjoram
3 oz. beef suet, finely chopped	10 oz. flour
½ onion, grated	1 egg
1 clove garlic, finely chopped	water
salt	broth or salted water

Put the meat in a bowl. Add the suet, grated onion, garlic and salt. Mix well. Season with salt and pepper and add marjoram. Stir in 2–3 tablespoons water and stir until well blended. Sift the flour and put it in a bowl. Make a well in the centre and break in the egg. Add salt and enough cold water to make a pliable dough. Roll out thinly and cut into small rounds or squares. Place a teaspoon of the meat mixture in the centre of each round or square and press the edges together. Make sure the ravioli is firmly sealed to prevent it from opening. Bring the broth or salted water to the boil and drop in the ravioli. Cook for about 10 minutes, drain and serve. If you have used broth, serve in the broth.

Ravioli: Vareniki
(*Ukrainian*)

12 oz. flour	4 oz. cottage cheese
1–2 eggs	½ small onion, chopped
salt	1 oz. butter
water	salt
1 lb. potatoes	pepper

Sift the flour and salt into a bowl. Make a well in the centre and break an egg into it. Add enough lukewarm water to make a dough which is not too stiff. Roll the dough out on a floured board and cut into rounds about 2½ inches in diameter.

Heat some butter in a frying-pan and fry the onion until golden brown. Peel, boil and mash the potatoes. Add the onion to the potato. Also add the cheese, salt and pepper and mix well. Place a teaspoon of the potato mixture in the centre of each pastry round and bring edges together, sealing them firmly. (Damp edges with a little water to make sealing more secure.)

Heat a saucepan of boiling salted water and drop in the ravioli. Cook for about 3 minutes or until they float to the top. Take out of the saucepan and place on a hot serving dish. Serve with a little browned melted butter poured over them.

Ravioli with mushrooms: zrazi z grzybami
(*Polish*)

8 oz. flour	½ onion, chopped
1 egg	1 oz. butter
salt	pepper
water	1 egg
12 oz. mushrooms, sliced	1 tablesp. dried breadcrumbs

Sift the flour and salt into a bowl. Make a hollow in the centre and drop in the beaten egg. Mix, gradually adding a little water to make a soft and pliable dough. Divide in half. Roll out one half thinly, covering the other half with a plate to prevent it from going dry. Cut the rolled-out dough into small rounds or squares and put a teaspoon of the filling in the centre. Press the edges of the rounds together and fold the squares into triangles. Seal the edges firmly so that the filling will not come out. Follow the same procedure with the second half of dough.

Bring a large saucepan of salted water to the boil and drop in the ravioli one at a time. Cover the pan and bring to the boil again. When the ravioli floats to the top remove the lid and cook for 3 minutes. Take out of the water and place on a hot dish. Serve with fried breadcrumbs.

To make filling: Heat the butter in a pan and sauté lightly the chopped onion. Add the mushrooms and a little water and cook until the mushrooms are ready and the water nearly evaporated. Season with salt and pepper and add the breadcrumbs and the beaten egg. Mix well.

Spaghetti with peas: Piselli
(*Italian*)

8 oz. spaghetti	salt
2 tablesp. olive oil	pepper
1 small onion, chopped	butter
8 oz. cooked green peas	grated Parmesan cheese
3 oz. cooked ham	

Cook the spaghetti in a large saucepan full of boiling salted water for about 15 minutes. Drain well and place on a hot dish. Heat the olive oil in a frying-pan and fry the onion, but do not brown. Add the peas, ham, salt and pepper. Mix the spaghetti with this and return to the hot dish. Serve covered with grated cheese and knobs of butter.

Steamed dumplings: Momo
(*Tibetan*)

8 oz. plain flour	*For filling:*
6 tablesp. tepid water (approx.)	8 oz. minced beef or pork
2 teasp. oil	½ teasp. ve-tsin
	½ teasp. salt
	1 tablesp. oil
	½ onion, chopped
	½ inch fresh ginger, chopped
	2 teasp. soya sauce
	1 tablesp. boiling water

Sift the flour and mix with the tepid water and 2 teaspoons oil to make a soft dough. Knead well and roll into a long sausage about 1 inch thick. Cut into 1-inch-long pieces and roll out each piece into a thin round.

Place the minced meat in a bowl, add the rest of the ingredients and mix well.

Place a heaped teaspoonful of this filling in the centre of each round, and pinch together the edges.

Cover the bottom of a steamer with a piece of wet muslin and arrange the dumplings on the cloth, leaving a space between them. Steam, covered, over boiling water for about 20 minutes.

Stuffed pancakes
(*Chinese*)

6 oz. flour	*For filling:*
1 egg	2 tablesp. oil
1½ cups water	1 lb. minced pork
oil for frying	1 leek or ½ small onion, chopped
pork fat	2 teasp. fresh ginger, chopped
	1 tablesp. wine or sherry

Beat the egg with water and gradually add the flour. Mix well to obtain a thin batter. Leave to stand for 30 minutes. Grease a 7-inch tin with a piece of pork fat held on a fork and heat it. Pour the batter in to form a thin pancake and leave to set. Remove from the pan. Repeat until all the batter has been used. Place a small amount of filling on each pancake, fold sides and roll. To secure edges seal them with a little cornflour blended with water. Fry the pancakes in hot oil until brown and crisp.

To prepare the filling: Heat oil in a pan and sauté the chopped onion or leek lightly. Add the meat and ginger, and fry quickly to brown the meat. Add the soya sauce and wine and mix well.

DISHES MADE WITH RICE

Chinese method of cooking rice

2 cups rice   3 cups water

Put the rice in a saucepan and add water. Bring to the boil and cook until the water has been absorbed. Next, if cooking by gas, turn flame down as low as possible; if cooking by electricity, turn off power and leave rice to dry out in saucepan.

Indian method of cooking rice

1 lb. Patna or Busmati rice   2 teasp. salt
5–6 pints water

Bring water and salt to the boil in a large saucepan. Boil rapidly for 10–15 minutes. Drain the rice in a large colander and pour boiling water over it. Place on an ovenproof dish and put in a cool oven to dry.

Aubergine pilau: Brinjal pilau
(*Indian*)

2 large onions   3 cups rice
4 medium-sized aubergines   ¼ teasp. cumin seeds
1 teasp. turmeric   8 cloves
6 dry red chillies, ground   a few cardamoms
4 tablesp. oil or ghee   salt to taste

Heat 2 tablespoons oil or ghee in a saucepan. Chop the onion and sauté in the fat. Peel the aubergines and cut into 1-inch pieces. Add them to the onion and season with salt. Add the red chilli powder and cook on a very low heat until the aubergines are tender.

Wash the rice and drain. Chop the second onion. Heat rest of fat in another pan. Fry the onion in it but do not brown. Add the rice, cumin seeds, cloves, cardamoms and salt. Sauté this mixture for a while. Add 2 cups water and cook on a low heat. Add more water in small quantities as required until the rice is tender. 15 minutes before serving, add the cooked aubergines. Cover the pan and finish cooking over a very low heat.

Bagdad pilau
(*Iraqi*)

1 medium-sized chicken	a few cardamoms
1 lb. rice	4 oz. sultanas
4 oz. oil	salt
1½ onions	1 lb. flour
1 teasp. turmeric powder	4 oz. butter (or oil)
1 stick cinnamon	water

Put the chicken in a saucepan. Season with salt, cover with water and add ½ an onion. Bring to boil, skim, cover the pan and simmer on a low heat until the chicken is tender. Remove from the pan and reserve the stock.

In a separate saucepan heat 4 oz. oil and sauté lightly the chopped onion. Add the turmeric, cinnamon and cardamoms and stir for a few minutes. Add the rice and fry, stirring for a minute or two. Add sufficient chicken stock to cover the rice and fill the saucepan to a depth of 1 inch above the rice. If there is not enough stock, add water. Season with salt. Cover the pan and simmer until the liquid has been absorbed. Add sultanas and mix well.

Rub the butter into the flour mixed with a little salt in a bowl. Add enough cold water to make a firm dough. Knead well, roll out thinly on a floured board and line a greased, deep ovenproof dish or baking tin with the dough. Remove the skin and bones from the chicken and put alternate layers of chicken pieces and pilau in the dish or tin until all has been used up. Cover the top with paste and seal the edges well. Dot the top with butter and cook in a moderate oven till top is brown, and dough cooked.

Chicken pilau
(*Indian*)

1 chicken weighing 2 lb.	2 oz. sultanas
1 lb. rice	½ small onion
1 large onion, chopped	2 hard-boiled eggs, cut into
1 stick cinnamon, 2 inches long	quarters
10 cloves	1 large onion, sliced thinly and
6 cardamoms	fried crisp
2 oz. blanched almonds, sliced	water

Put the chicken in a pan, season with salt and cover with cold water.

Bring to the boil and skim. Add half the onion and simmer until the chicken is tender. Strain the liquid and keep it on one side. Wash the rice, soak in cold water and drain. Heat the oil in a pan and sauté lightly the rest of the chopped onion, add the rice and spices and fry for a few minutes, stirring continuously. Add the chicken stock. Cover the rice with the stock and let it reach a depth of 1–2 inches above the rice. If there is not enough stock, add water. Cover the saucepan and bring contents to the boil, reduce heat and simmer on a low heat until the liquid has been absorbed and the rice cooked.

Fry the sliced almonds and sultanas in a pan and add to the rice. Mix well and serve on a heated dish. Place the jointed chicken on top and garnish with hard-boiled eggs and fried onion.

Dubrovnik rice
(*Dalmatian*)

2 oz. butter or lard	1 tablesp. tomato purée diluted
1 medium-sized onion, chopped	in 4 cups stock
3 oz. smoked pork fat or bacon	salt
cut into small cubes	pepper
1 lb. rice	grated cheese

Heat butter or lard in a pan and sauté the chopped onion for a few minutes. Add the pork or bacon and the rice. Season with salt and pepper and continue frying without browning the rice. Gradually add the stock with the tomato purée. Cook slowly, stirring the rice frequently. Add more stock during the cooking if necessary. Cook until rice is soft and liquid absorbed. Serve on a dish with grated cheese sprinkled on top.

Fried rice: Chow farn
(*Chinese*)

1½ tablesp. oil	3 cups cold cooked rice
2 beaten eggs	chopped spring onions
salt	2 teasp. soya sauce

Heat oil in a frying-pan, add beaten eggs, season with salt and stir until the egg is nearly set. Add the cold rice and continue frying. Add the chopped onions and soya sauce. Stir until the rice is thoroughly heated and serve. Chopped fried bacon, cooked ham or mushrooms can be added.

K

Moulmein rice
(*Burmese*)

2 cups rice

3 onions, sliced

8 cloves garlic, chopped

2 tablesp. red chilli powder

$\frac{3}{4}$ cup oil

$\frac{1}{2}$ cup shredded dried salt fish

30 dried prawns, powdered

Boil the rice and set aside. Heat the oil in a pan and fry the garlic and 2 sliced onions. When brown remove from the pan and set aside. In the same oil, fry the red chilli powder for 1–2 minutes, add the boiled rice and mix well. This will give the rice a pleasant red colour. Put rice on a serving dish and surround with dried prawn powder, fried onions, 1 sliced raw onion, fried garlic and shredded salt fish.

Mutton pilau with buriani
(*Arabian*)

2 lb. mutton or lamb

2 onions, finely chopped

3 cloves garlic, finely chopped

1 inch fresh ginger, chopped or ground

1 teasp. poppy seeds

1 tablesp. curry powder

1 tablesp. garam masala

2 tablesp. cumin powder

2 tablesp. coriander powder

4 oz. oil or ghee

1 lb. rice

1 cup curd

1 teasp. saffron

1 dessertsp. salt or to taste

8 green chillies, sliced

a few fresh coriander leaves

For the buriani:

1 lb. curd

1 teasp. chopped mint leaves

2 tablesp. chopped coriander leaves

2 teasp. chopped green chillies

Cut meat into fairly large cubes and simmer in sufficient water to cover the meat. Cook till meat is almost tender.

Soak the rice in cold water for about 30 minutes and drain. Heat the oil or ghee in a deep pan and fry lightly the chopped onions, garlic and ginger. Add all the other spices and continue frying for about 5 minutes. Stir in the rice and fry for a few minutes, add the curd, saffron, green chillies, coriander leaves, salt and meat cubes. Pour over it the boiling stock in which the mutton was cooked until it covers the rice by an inch. Cover the pan and cook slowly until the rice is cooked and the meat tender.

To prepare the buriani: Drain liquid from the curd and mix with the chopped mint, coriander powder and chillies. Serve with the pilau.

Rice with cherries: Albaloo polo
(*Persian*)

1 lb. rice	1 lb. sour red or black cherries
4 oz. salt	with sugar and water for cooking
4 oz. butter	or
½ cup hot water	1 lb. tinned cherries

Wash the rice and soak overnight in lukewarm water and salt. The water should cover the rice.

Fill a large pan with water and bring to the boil. Drain and rinse the rice and add to the boiling water. Boil rapidly, removing the scum forming on top, until rice is half cooked, and drain. If the rice is too salty, rinse with lukewarm water.

Melt the butter in a pan and mix with ½ cup hot water. Pour half of the butter mixture into a cup and keep aside.

Boil the cherries in a saucepan with water and sugar. Drain and stone. (If tinned cherries are used, do not boil, but drain them.) Mix the cherries with the half-cooked rice.

Heat half of the water and butter mixture in a saucepan and add the rice with cherries. Pour the remaining water and butter over the rice and make a dent on top of the rice. Place a knob of butter in the dent, cover the pan with a cloth and place a lid on top. Cook over low heat until all water has been absorbed (about 12–15 minutes).

Serve the rice with meat or chicken.

Rice with chicken: Pish-pash
(*Indian*)

1 medium-sized chicken	1 bay leaf
10 oz. rice	salt
2 tablesp. oil or ghee	pepper
1 large chopped onion	3 pints stock or water
1 teasp. turmeric powder	

Cut the chicken into quarters. Wash and drain the rice. In a deep saucepan, heat the oil or ghee and sauté lightly the onion without browning it. Add the turmeric and stir for 1–2 minutes. Add the chicken pieces and turn them once or twice. Add the rice and bay leaf. Season with salt and pepper. Cover with stock or water (preferably chicken stock) and simmer on a low heat until chicken is tender and rice is creamy (about 1½–2 hours). Cover the saucepan whilst the contents are simmering. The rice should never be allowed to go dry so more stock may be added, if needed, during the cooking. This dish can also be cooked in the oven.

Risotto Milanese
(*Italian*)

2 oz. butter or	½ teasp. saffron
1 oz. butter and	¼ cup dry white wine
1 tablesp. oil	2 pints chicken stock
1 onion, chopped	3 oz. grated Parmesan cheese
12 oz. rice (Italian)	knob butter
salt	

Heat the fat in a pan and sauté lightly the onion, but do not brown. Add the rice and stir till it is well buttered but still white. Blend the saffron with the wine and pour onto rice. Cook, stirring all the time, until the liquid has been absorbed. Gradually add the hot stock. Stir frequently and simmer on a low heat for about 30 minutes, when the rice should be done. The rice should be soft but firm. (Add more water, if necessary.) Season to taste and stir in 1 oz. grated cheese and a knob of butter. Serve the rest of the cheese separately in a bowl.
Note: This is a basic risotto to which almost anything can be added, such as mushrooms, chicken, shellfish, chicken livers or vegetables. Add these during the last 10 minutes cooking time.

Spanish rice: Arroz español
(*Spanish*)

8 oz. rice	2½ cups stock
3 tablesp. olive oil	3 skinned tomatoes or
1 small onion, chopped	2 tablesp. tomato purée
1 clove garlic	salt
3 oz. streaky bacon, cut into small	pepper
pieces	6 oz. cooked or tinned green peas

Heat the oil in a pan and sauté lightly the onion and crushed garlic for a few minutes. Add the bacon and rice and continue frying, but do not brown. Add the tomatoes or tomato purée and season to taste. Add

the hot stock and bring all to the boil. Cover the pan and place in a
pre-heated oven 350° F., Gas reg. 4, for 30–40 minutes, until rice is
tender and liquid absorbed. Drain the peas and mix with rice.

Serve garnished with strips of red pepper.

White rice: Chalow
(Afghanistan)

1 lb. rice	1 teasp. cumin seed powder
2 oz. ghee or butter	water
1 teasp. salt	

Wash the rice and place in a deep pan. Cover with water and leave to
soak for several hours.

Fill another pan with water, add salt and bring to the boil. Drain
rice and add it to the boiling water. Cook until soft but firm (10–12
minutes). Drain and rinse in cold water.

Put rice in a pan. Melt the butter or ghee in ½ cup of hot water and
sprinkle it lightly over the rice together with the cumin seed powder.
Make a few holes in the rice to allow the steam to escape. Cover the
pan and finish cooking in a cool oven.

Poultry Dishes

Chicken

Chicken à la Kiev (*Russian*)
Chicken and vegetable curry
 (*Indonesian*)
Chicken breasts (*Italian*)
Chicken casserole (*Belgian*)
Chicken chakhobili (*Circassian*)
Chicken chartarnee (*Middle East*)
Chicken Imperial (*Austrian*)
Chicken Karachi (*Pakistani*)
Chicken pie (*Russian*)
Chicken shashlik (*Pakistani*)
Chicken tandoori (*Punjabi*)
Chicken with beer (*Alsatian*)

Chicken with dill sauce
 (*Czechoslovakian*)
Chicken with mushrooms
 (*Austrian*)
Chicken with mushrooms
 (*Chinese*)
Chicken with prunes (*Persian*)
Chicken with tomatoes
 (*Middle East*)
Poulet à la Villeroi (*French*)
Spiced chicken livers (*Pakistani*)
Spring chickens (*Polish*)
Stuffed chicken (*Persian*)
Stuffed roast chicken (*Malaysian*)

Duck

Chinese braised duck (*Chinese*)
Duck with apples (*Polish*)
Duck with brown sauce (*German*)
Duck with orange (*French*)

Duck with red cabbage (*Polish*)
Duck with turnips (*French*)
Spiced fried duck (*Chinese*)

CHICKEN

Chicken à la Kiev
(*Russian*)

1 chicken breast per person	salt
maître d'hôtel butter	pepper
eggs	oil for frying
dried breadcrumbs	

Skin and bone the chicken breasts, leaving half the wing to form a 'handle'. Scrape the meat from the wing towards the breast. Beat the chicken with the back of the knife, flatten and form into cutlets. Season with salt and pepper. Put a finger-sized piece of very cold *maître d'hotel* butter on each piece of chicken and carefully roll the breast towards the bone, shaping it like a rissole. Dip in flour, then in the beaten eggs which have been thinned with a little water, and finally in breadcrumbs. Repeat this once more.

Heat the oil in a deep pan and fry the chicken over a slow heat until it is golden brown and cooked through.

Note: Maître d'hotel butter is made by creaming 4 oz. fresh butter with a little lemon juice, chopped parsley, salt and a few drops of Worcester sauce. Keep very cold. It is also advisable to put the prepared chicken in the refrigerator for 1 hour before frying, to enable the egg and breadcrumbs to set.

Chicken and vegetable curry
(*Indonesian*)

1 medium-sized chicken	2 large boiled carrots
2 tablesp. oil or ghee	2 stalks boiled celery
2 medium-sized onions, finely sliced	2 spring onions, cut in pieces
2 cloves garlic, crushed	2 potatoes, sliced
1 inch fresh ginger, finely chopped	2 hard-boiled eggs
1 teasp. red chilli powder	2 teasp. lemon juice
salt	2 cups water

Heat the ghee or oil in a pan and sauté the sliced onion until golden in colour. Add the garlic, chicken cut into quarters, ginger and chilli powder. Season with salt and fry for a few minutes. Add 2 cups water. Cover the pan and simmer until chicken is tender.

Heat some oil or ghee in a frying-pan and fry the potatoes. When the chicken is cooked, serve the quarters in individual dishes with portions of potatoes, vegetables and hard-boiled egg. Add the lemon juice to the stock and pour over the meat and vegetables.

Chicken breasts: Petti di pollo
(*Italian*)

2 chicken breasts	½ cup chicken stock
1½ oz. butter	¼ cup white wine
4 slices Mozzarella cheese (or	1 tablesp. brandy
any mild cheese)	salt
a few sliced mushrooms	pepper

Skin and bone the chicken breasts. Each breast will divide naturally into one large and one small fillet. Flatten fillets by pounding them with a mallet between two pieces of waxed paper. Heat the butter in a pan. Dip the chicken fillets in the flour and put them into the hot fat. Cook slowly for 5 minutes on each side. Remove them from the pan and put them on a hot dish. Add sliced mushrooms to the fat in the pan and sauté for a few minutes. Add wine, chicken stock and brandy and bring to the boil. Return the chicken fillets to the pan, season with salt and pepper, and put a slice of cheese on each. Cover the pan and simmer for a few minutes until the cheese has melted.

Chicken casserole: Poulet cocotte
(*Belgian*)

1 chicken, weighing 3 lb.	1 sliced celery stalk
3 oz. butter	10 shallots
2 rashers bacon, diced	8 oz. sliced mushrooms
salt	bouquet garni
pepper	water
2 diced carrots	

Cut the chicken into quarters and season with salt and pepper. Heat half the butter in a large pan and brown the chicken pieces in it. Add the bacon and a little hot water. Cover the pan and simmer for 20 minutes.

Melt rest of the butter in another pan and sauté the onion lightly for about 10 minutes, add carrots and celery and stir. Add the vegetables to the chicken, together with the mushrooms and bouquet garni. Cover the pan and continue cooking on a low heat until the meat is tender.

Chicken chakhobili
(Circassian)

1 medium-sized chicken	1 oz. cooking fat
1 clove garlic, chopped	3 tablesp. tomato purée
2 teasp. lemon juice	1 wine glass of white wine
salt	½ cup chicken stock (made with
1 large onion, chopped	giblets)

Quarter the chicken and rub with garlic and salt. Sprinkle lemon juice over the pieces and leave for 1 hour. Heat fat in pan and sauté the chopped onion lightly. Add the chicken and brown slightly, then add the tomato purée and wine. Bring to the boil and add hot stock. Cover the pan and simmer until chicken is done and stock is reduced to half its former quantity.

Chicken chartarnee
(Middle East)

1 chicken, weighing 2 lb.	8 cloves
2 cloves garlic	4 cardamoms
2 chillies	3 tablesp. tomato purée
1 teasp. turmeric powder	a few coriander leaves
1 onion, sliced	2 teasp. lemon juice
1 dessertsp. cumin seeds	oil for frying
salt	water

Grind the garlic with the chillies and mix with the turmeric powder. Heat oil in a pan and fry the onions slowly, but do not allow them to brown. Add the ground ingredients, the cumin seeds, cloves and cardamoms, and continue frying for a few minutes. Add the chicken cut into quarters, the coriander leaves and tomato purée. Add a little water, cover the pan and simmer until the chicken is done. Add the lemon juice just before the end of the cooking time. Serve chicken with rice.

Chicken Imperial
(Austrian)

A recipe from the chef to the Royal Court of Vienna.

1 medium-sized chicken	2 eggs
salt	1 egg yolk
pepper	grated Parmesan cheese
2 oz. butter	butter
1 cup cream	dried breadcrumbs
½ tablesp. flour	

Quarter the chicken, sprinkle with salt and leave it for 30 minutes. Heat the butter in a pan and sauté the chicken until nearly done. Cover the pan when the chicken is in it. Transfer the cooked chicken pieces into an ovenproof dish and sprinkle with grated Parmesan cheese and pepper.

In a small saucepan, blend the cream and flour and bring to the boil. Season with salt and remove from the heat. Beat the eggs with the additional egg yolk and add to the cream. Mix well and pour over the chicken. Sprinkle with Parmesan cheese and breadcrumbs and dot with butter. Bake in a moderately hot oven for 20 minutes or until a golden crust has formed.

Chicken Karachi: Karachi ka murghi
(Pakistani)

1 small chicken	2–3 eggs, beaten
2 inch fresh ginger	dried breadcrumbs
5 cloves garlic	ghee or oil for deep frying
salt	water

Rub the chicken inside and out with salt. Grind the ginger and garlic into a paste and spread it all over the chicken. Put the chicken into a pan and add enough water to cover the bird. Put a lid on the saucepan and, after bringing liquid to the boil, simmer until the chicken is tender. Remove chicken from the pan and cool slightly. Roll whole chicken in beaten eggs and breadcrumbs. Heat fat in a deep frying-pan and put chicken in. Fry until chicken is golden brown in colour.

Chicken pie: Kournik
(*Russian*)

8 oz. flour
½ oz. yeast
½ teasp. sugar
1 oz. butter
1 egg
¼ cup milk

2 chicken breasts or ½ chicken,
   boiled or steamed
4 oz. boiled mushrooms
2 hard-boiled eggs, sliced
½ pint thick white sauce
salt
pepper

Sieve flour and salt into a bowl and rub in the fat. Make a hollow in the centre and pour in the yeast, creamed with sugar and a tablespoon of warmed milk. Sprinkle a little flour over the yeast and leave in a warm place to rise. Add the rest of the warmed milk and beaten egg. Mix and knead until the dough leaves the hands clean. Cover with a cloth and leave in a warm place until the dough has doubled its size.

Bone the chicken and cut meat into cubes. Mix with half the white sauce. Slice the mushrooms and stir them into the rest of the white sauce.

Grease and flour a deep pie dish. Roll out three-quarters of the dough and line the pie dish with it. Place alternate layers of chicken, mushrooms and sliced eggs in the pie dish and repeat until the dish is full. Roll out the rest of the dough and cover the dish. Leave for 30–45 minutes to rise. Cook in a pre-heated oven at 400° F., Gas reg. 6 for 45 minutes or until the pastry is brown. Turn out and serve.

Chicken shashlik: Shashlik murgh
(*Pakistani*)

1 medium-sized chicken
1 cup yoghurt
3 cloves garlic, finely chopped
1 inch fresh ginger, finely chopped
1 dessertsp. coriander powder
1 teasp. mustard

½ teasp. turmeric powder
½ teasp. red chilli powder
1 teasp. garam masala
½ lb. tomatoes
½ lb. green peppers
ghee or oil for basting

Bone the chicken and cut the meat into cubes. Pour the yoghurt into a bowl and mix with the garlic, ginger, coriander, salt, mustard, turmeric, chilli powder and garam masala. (Pound spices with the garlic before adding to the yoghurt.) Put the chicken pieces in this mixture and leave for 2 hours or longer.

Cut the tomatoes and peppers into pieces. Put chicken pieces on a skewer with tomatoes and peppers and grill over a charcoal fire or under an ordinary grill, basting frequently with ghee or oil.

Chicken tandoori: Tandoori murghi
(*Punjabi*)

1 medium-sized chicken	2 teasp. 'tandoori powder' or
1 inch fresh ginger, finely chopped	sweet Hungarian paprika
1 teasp. garam masala	4 cloves garlic, finely chopped
salt	4 oz. yoghurt
	2 oz. ghee or oil

Pound ginger, garlic, garam masala and salt. Mix with yoghurt. Rub chicken with tandoori powder or paprika to give it a rich red colour, pour the yoghurt mixture over the chicken and leave for several hours.

Heat the fat in a roasting tin and put the chicken in it. Pour the yoghurt mixture over the bird. Roast in a pre-heated, moderately hot oven for about 1 hour, or until the bird is tender and a rich red colour. Baste frequently during the roasting.

Chicken with beer
(*Alsatian*)

1 medium-sized chicken	salt
2 oz. butter, or oil and butter	pepper
mixed	¾ cup beer
1 large onion, chopped	2–3 tablesp. double cream

Cut the chicken into four pieces and put in a pan to brown slightly in hot butter, or butter mixed with oil. Remove chicken pieces from pan and in the same hot fat sauté the chopped onion until golden in colour. Return the chicken pieces to the pan with fried onion, season with salt and pepper and cover with beer. Cover the pan and simmer the chicken on a low heat until tender (about 1 hour). When the chicken is ready, place on a hot serving dish and keep warm. Add a little of the hot chicken stock to the cream, mix well and pour into the gravy in the pan. Bring to the boil, then pour the sauce over the chicken.

Chicken with dill sauce
(*Czechoslovakian*)

1 chicken, weighing 3 lb.
salt
flour
1½ oz. butter

For the sauce:
1 oz. butter
1 oz. flour
½ pint chicken broth
½ cup double cream
2 tablesp. chopped fresh dill
lemon juice

Quarter the chicken, sprinkle with salt and leave for 1 hour. Sprinkle the chicken quarters with flour. Heat butter in a pan and fry the chicken on both sides. Lower the heat and add a little water. Cover the pan and simmer until the chicken is tender. If needed, more water can be added but care must be taken not to have too much liquid in the pan.

To prepare the sauce: In a saucepan, melt 1 oz. butter and make a roux with the flour. Gradually add the chicken broth. Stir until well blended and the sauce thickens.

Pour the sauce over the chicken in the pan and simmer for a few minutes. Stir to prevent the chicken pieces from sticking to the pan. Add the cream and the chopped dill. Bring to the boil and remove from the heat. Add the lemon juice, stir and serve with boiled rice.

Chicken with mushrooms: Huhn mit Schwammerln
(*Austrian*)

1 medium-sized chicken
1 lb. mushrooms, sliced
3 oz. melted butter
salt

pepper
chopped parsley
1 teasp. flour

Quarter the chicken and slice the mushrooms. Butter an ovenproof dish well and arrange half the sliced mushrooms on the bottom. Put the chicken pieces on top and cover with the rest of the mushrooms. Season each layer with salt and pepper. Pour melted butter over the mushrooms and chicken. Cover the dish and bake in a moderate oven for 30–40 minutes or until the chicken is tender.

Blend the flour with a little cold water and add to the liquid in the dish. Stir well and then put the dish in the oven again for a few minutes. Sprinkle with chopped parsley and serve.

Chicken with mushrooms
(*Chinese*)

1 small chicken	1 teasp. sugar
6 oz. dried Chinese mushrooms (soaked in water)	2 tablesp. white wine or sherry
	3 tablesp. soya sauce
1 inch fresh ginger, chopped or crushed	oil for frying

Cut the chicken into 8 pieces and rub with salt. Remove the stalks from the mushrooms and soak the mushrooms in water for several hours. Heat the oil in a pan and put the chicken pieces in it. Fry until they are well browned. Add the drained mushrooms and the ginger. Continue frying. Mix the sugar, soya sauce, wine (or sherry) and a little of the water in which the mushrooms have been soaking and pour over the chicken. Cover the pan and simmer gently until the chicken is tender.

Chicken with prunes
(*Persian*)

1 medium-sized chicken	1 dessertsp. sugar
½ lb. prunes	½ teasp. cinnamon
2 oz. cooking fat	½ teasp. turmeric powder
1 large onion, sliced	salt
1½ cups water	

Cut the chicken into several pieces and soak the prunes for an hour. Drain the prunes. Heat some fat in a pan and fry the onion until golden in colour. Take the onion from the pan and put aside. In the same pan, fry the chicken pieces until light brown, then add the onion. Season with salt, add sugar, spices and prunes. Stirring all the time, add in 1½ cups hot water. Cover the pan and cook on a medium heat until the chicken is tender and the fat floats to the top and can be removed.

Serve with boiled rice.

Chicken with tomatoes
(*Middle East*)

1 medium-sized chicken	½ teasp. turmeric powder
1 inch fresh ginger, ground	salt
2 cloves garlic, ground	pepper
1 tablesp. oil	3 large tomatoes, sliced
1 large onion, sliced	water

Cut the chicken into half and cut each half into three pieces. Heat the oil in a pan and fry the ginger and garlic. Add the onion and turmeric. Stir for 1–2 minutes, then add chicken and tomatoes. Season with salt. Add a little hot water. Cover the pan and cook slowly until chicken is tender.

Serve with boiled rice.

Poulet à la Villeroi
(French)

1 young chicken, weighing 2 lb.	1 oz. flour
a knob butter	¾ cup stock
½ onion	3–4 tablesp. cream
1 carrot	1 egg yolk
1 small piece celery	fat for frying
salt	dried breadcrumbs
1 oz. butter	

Put the chicken in a pan with the onion, carrot, celery and butter. Season with salt and add enough water to prevent it sticking to the pan. Keep adding a little water as necessary. Cook chicken until tender, remove it from the pan to a dish and strain the stock. Cut chicken into quarters.

Make a roux with 1 oz. butter and flour. Slowly add the chicken stock, stirring all the time. When the sauce has thickened add cream and salt and cook for 1 minute. Remove from the heat and add the egg yolk. (If sauce is too thick, add a little more cream or stock. If not thick enough, cook longer.)

Dip chicken pieces in the sauce. Lift pieces out with a fork and hold them in the air so that the sauce congeals on the pieces. Then dip in breadcrumbs. Heat some fat in a frying-pan. Put in the coated chicken pieces and fry till golden brown. Garnish with fried parsley.

Spiced chicken livers: Murghi kaleji
(Pakistani)

½ lb. chicken livers	2 cloves
2 tablesp. ghee or oil	½ teasp. garam masala
1 medium-sized onion, chopped	½ teasp. turmeric powder
3 green chillies, sliced finely	½ teasp. cumin seed powder
1 ripe tomato, chopped	salt

Heat the ghee or oil in a pan and fry the chopped onion and cloves.

L

Add the spices and the chicken livers, and brown them well. Add the tomato, season with salt and simmer until the liver is cooked and the fat floats to the top.

Spring chickens: Mlode kurczeta po polsku
(*Polish*)

2 spring chickens	2 tablesp. chopped, fresh dill
salt	pepper
3 oz. white rolls	a pinch sugar
¼ cup milk	3 oz. butter for roasting
1 oz. butter	1–2 tablesp. dried breadcrumbs
2 eggs	(if necessary)

Clean the chickens and rub with salt inside and out. Leave for 1 hour. Soak the bread rolls in milk until soft. Squeeze slightly and mash. Separate the egg yolks and the whites.

Cream 1 oz. butter with the egg yolks. Add this to the softened rolls with the chopped dill, sugar, salt and pepper. Mix until well blended. Whip the egg whites, and fold into the mixture. If stuffing is now too soft, stir in 1–2 tablespoons dried breadcrumbs.

Stuff the chickens with this mixture, putting some of the stuffing under the skin over the breast and the rest inside the chickens. Secure the opening with skewers. Heat the butter in a roasting tin and put the chickens in it. Cook in a pre-heated oven at 400° F., Gas reg. 6, for about 1 hour, basting frequently. When the chickens are cooked, remove from the pan, cut into halves and pour the fat from the roasting tin over them. Garnish with fried parsley.

Serve with fresh lettuce, new potatoes and cucumber salad.

Stuffed chicken: Beryane morgh
(*Persian*)

1 chicken weighing 3 lb.	½ teasp. cinnamon
1½ oz. sultanas	2 oz. cooking fat
3 tablesp. cooked rice	2 tablesp. tomato purée
salt	1 cup hot water
pepper	

Rub chicken inside and out with salt and pepper. Heat 1 oz. of fat in a pan and fry the sultanas. Remove them from the pan. To the same fat add the chicken giblets, cut in small pieces, and fry for a few minutes. Take them out and mix them with the sultanas, rice and cinnamon. Season with salt and pepper. Stuff the chicken with this mixture. Close the opening in the chicken with a skewer to prevent the stuffing from coming out. Heat the rest of the fat and brown the chicken on all sides, add 1 cup of hot water and cover the pan. Simmer until the chicken is half done. Add the tomato purée. Continue cooking until the chicken is tender.

Stuffed roast chicken
(*Malaysian*)

1 large roasting chicken	½ teasp. coriander powder
½–1 cup rice	¼ teasp. cloves
2 oz. sultanas	2 cloves garlic, crushed
2 oz. currants	1 teasp. chilli powder
¼ cup shredded almonds	1½ oz. butter or ghee
½ inch chopped fresh ginger	salt
5 cardamoms	saffron

Boil the rice with a pinch of saffron and cool. Chop the chicken liver. Heat some ghee or butter in a pan and lightly fry the liver. Add the sultanas, currants and almonds. Stir. Add the rice, cardamoms, coriander, cloves, ginger, garlic and chilli powder. Season with salt and fry for a few minutes, stirring so that the mixture becomes well blended. Add more fat if necessary. Take off the heat.

Fill the chicken with the stuffing and secure the opening with skewers. Truss the chicken and place breast down on a baking dish. Bake in a pre-heated moderate oven, 375° F., Gas reg. 5, for 30 minutes. Turn the chicken over and finish roasting, basting frequently until the chicken is tender, approximately 30 minutes.

DUCK

Chinese braised duck
(*Chinese*)

1 duck weighing 3 lb.
1 inch fresh ginger, chopped finely
2 tablesp. wine or sherry
1 clove garlic, chopped finely

4 tablesp. oil
4 tablesp. soya sauce
2 leeks, sliced
2 cups hot water

Cut the duck in 4 pieces and rub each piece with a mixture of chopped ginger, garlic and wine or sherry. Allow to stand for 30 minutes. Heat the oil in a pan and fry the duck until brown, remove from the pan and drain. Place the fried duck in a heavy pan. Add soya sauce, sugar, sliced leeks and hot water. Bring to boil and simmer (covered) for about 1–1½ hours or until tender.

Duck with apples: Kaczka z jablkami
(*Polish*)

1 large duck
1–2 lb. cooking apples
salt

marjoram
1 oz. butter or cooking fat

Rub duck with salt inside and out. Sprinkle with pepper and marjoram and allow to stand for 1 hour. Peel the apples, quarter them and remove core. Stuff the bird with the apples and secure the opening with skewers. Place bird in a roasting pan and pour melted fat over it. Sprinkle with cold water. Bake in a pre-heated oven at 450° F., Gas reg. 8, for 5 minutes, then lower heat to 350° F., Gas reg. 4, and cook slowly, basting frequently until duck is tender and browned. Cut the duck into four pieces. Place on a hot serving dish and garnish with cooked apples.

Serve with white or red cabbage or cooked beetroot.

Note: You may use goose instead of duck in this recipe.

Duck with brown sauce: Gedampfte Ente in brauner Sauce
(German)

1 duckling	1 oz. butter
1 oz. butter	1 tablesp. flour
salt	½–1 glass red wine
pepper	½ teasp. sugar
2 cups hot water	¼ teasp. ground cloves
1 large onion	

In a large pan melt 1 oz. butter. Put duckling in and brown quickly on all sides. Season with salt and pepper. Cut onion into quarters and put in the pan with the duckling. Add 2 cups hot water. Cover the pan and simmer the duckling slowly until it is tender.

Melt 1 oz. butter in a frying-pan and put the flour in it then blend in a little of the stock in which the duckling has been cooked. (Remove fat from stock first.) Add wine, sugar and cloves and bring to the boil.

Remove duckling from the pan and cut into reasonable portions. Put it back in the pan and pour the sauce over it, adding enough of the stock to make a thick rich gravy. Cover the pan and simmer for a few minutes longer. Take duckling out of pan. Place on a serving dish and pour sauce over it.

Duck with orange: Canard à l'orange
(French)

1 duck weighing 4 lb.	pepper
1 orange	1 tablesp. red currant jelly
1 teasp. sugar	½ tablesp. flour
1 teasp. lemon juice	2 tablesp. Madeira
salt	

Put the duck in a roasting tin. Rub with salt and pepper and put in a hot oven 425° F., Gas reg. 7, for 10 minutes, reduce the heat to 375° F., Gas reg. 5. Continue to roast uncovered until the duck is tender. Baste frequently.

Skin the orange and scrape the pulp from the skin. Cut peel in thin strips. Simmer the orange peel in boiling water for 15 minutes and drain.

When the duck is cooked, remove from the pan. Pour off most of the fat and add ½ cup water. Blend the flour with a little of the juices in the pan. Add the sugar, lemon juice, orange juice and rind and simmer. Stir in the currant jelly and cook until the jelly dissolves. Add the Madeira.

Cut duck into serving portions and put on a serving dish. Pour over hot sauce and garnish with orange segments.

Duck with red cabbage: Kaczke z czerwona kapusta
(Polish)

1 duck weighing 3–4 lb.	½ tablesp. flour
2 lb. red cabbage	1 teasp. sugar
juice of 1 lemon	salt
2 oz. pork fat, cubed	pepper
½ onion, chopped	1 glass red wine

Shred the cabbage and plunge into boiling water for a minute. Drain and sprinkle with lemon juice. Fry the pork fat in a pan with the onion. Add the flour. Stir. Add the cabbage. Season with salt and pepper. Add sugar and wine.

Meanwhile put the duck in a roasting tin and roast in the oven. When it is half-cooked transfer it to the pan with the cabbage. Cover and simmer until the duck is tender.

Duck with turnips: Canard aux navets
(French)

1 duck weighing 3 lb.	a pinch of sugar
1½ oz. lard or cooking fat	1 tablesp. flour
1 lb. baby turnips	pepper
1 onion, chopped	¾ pint stock or water

Rub duck inside and out with salt and leave for 30 minutes. Heat lard in a large pan and brown duck. Remove duck from pan and keep it warm. Toss the turnips in the fat and sprinkle with sugar. Fry turnips until slightly browned and glazed, then take them out of the pan and keep them on one side. Fry the onion in the same fat. Add the flour, stirring all the time until flour is slightly brown, then gradually add the stock or water and bring to the boil, stirring continuously. Simmer for 10 minutes. Skim the fat which rises to the surface. Pass the sauce through a sieve and put it back in the pan. Bring it to the boil and add turnips and duck. Season with pepper and more salt if needed. Cover the pan and cook on a moderate heat for 1½ hours, or until duck is tender. Remove duck from pan and place on a hot serving dish. Arrange the turnips round it. Reduce gravy by boiling, remove surplus fat from the top and pour over the duck and turnips.

Spiced fried duck
(*Chinese*)

1 duckling	a pinch of powdered aniseed
2 tablesp. white wine or sherry	2 tablesp. soya sauce
salt	2 tablesp. honey or sugar
4 slices fresh ginger	oil for deep frying
1 leek	

Rub duckling with salt. Sprinkle with wine or sherry and allow to stand for 30 minutes. Put the duckling in a large steamer with the ginger and leek. Sprinkle with aniseed. Cover the bowl and put over a saucepan of boiling water. Steam until the duckling is tender (about 1½ hours). Remove duckling from the bowl and cool. Rub it well with soya sauce and honey or sugar. Heat fat in a deep frying-pan and fry duckling until it is crisp and brown.

SECTION NINE

Vegetable Dishes and Salads

Vegetable Dishes

Aubergine au gratin (*French*)

Aubergine fritter curry (*Pakistani*)

Aubergine in coconut milk (*Singhalese*)

Aubergine with mushrooms (*Polish*)

Fragrant aubergines (*Chinese*)

Mashed aubergines (*Punjabi*)

Bean sprouts and green peppers (*Chinese*)

Beetroot purée (*Dutch*)

Cauliflower with ham (*Serbian*)

Punjabi cauliflower (*Indian*)

Louvain carrots (*Belgian*)

Carrots in batter (*Polish*)

Carrots with butter (*Polish*)

Stuffed chicory (*Swiss*)

French beans (*Arabian*)

Green peas (*French*)

Mixed vegetables (*German*)

Mixed vegetables (*Gujurati*)

Flamed mushrooms (*French*)

Mushrooms and potatoes (*Polish*)

Mushrooms in sour cream (*Hungarian*)

Potato balls curry (*Indian*)

Potatoes in sour cream (*Russian*)

Potato omelette (*Spanish*)

Potato paprikash (*Hungarian*)

Potatoes stuffed with cheese (*Swiss*)

Potatoes with cheese (*French*)

Potatoes with ham (*German*)

Potatoes with onions (*German*)

Roast flaked potatoes (*Swiss*)

Ratatouille niçoise (*French*)

Red cabbage (*Polish*)

Sauerkraut with beans (*Swiss*)

Sauerkraut with salted cucumbers (*Russian*)

Sauerkraut (*German*)

Stuffed savoy cabbage (*Moravian*)

Stuffed marrows (*Punjabi*)

Gujurati tomatoes (*Indian*)

Tomatoes and green peppers (*Hungarian*)

Transylvanian beans (*Rumanian*)

Salads

Aubergine salad (*Indian*)
Aubergine salad (*Rumanian*)
Bean salad (*French*)
Celeriac salad (*French*)
Cheese salad (*German*)
Cucumber salad (*Danish*)
Fish salad (*Swiss*)
Green pepper salad (*Italian*)

Herring and potato salad
(*German*)
Mixed salad (*Indonesian*)
Onion salad with curd
(*Pakistani*)
Red cabbage salad (*Polish*)
Spinach with yoghurt (*Persian*)

VEGETABLE DISHES

Aubergine au gratin
(*French*)

I aubergine per person
I clove garlic, crushed
chopped parsley
butter

salt
pepper
dried breadcrumbs
grated Parmesan cheese

Cut the aubergines into halves. Melt some butter in a frying-pan and fry the aubergines until tender. Take out of the pan and scoop out the inside. Mash pulp with salt, pepper, garlic, chopped parsley and a teaspoon of melted butter for each aubergine. Refill the aubergine cases, cover with breadcrumbs, sprinkle with grated Parmesan cheese and dot with butter. Brown under the grill or in a hot oven.

Aubergine fritter curry
(*Pakistani*)

I large or 2 small aubergines,
  sliced
I large onion, finely chopped
2 cloves garlic, crushed
I inch fresh ginger, finely chopped
3 green chillies, halved
salt
I tablesp. vinegar
water

For the batter:
4 oz. besan flour (gram flour)
I egg
½ cup water
salt
ghee for deep frying

For garnish:
fresh coriander leaves

To prepare the batter: Put the flour and salt in a bowl, add the egg and gradually add the water. Mix to a thick batter. Beat until smooth. Dip aubergine slices in the batter. Heat fat in a deep frying-pan. Drop in aubergines and leave until brown and thoroughly cooked. Drain and keep aside.

In a separate saucepan, heat a little ghee and lightly fry the onion. Add the garlic, ginger, chillies, salt and vinegar. Add the water and cook until the gravy is thick. Add the fried aubergine slices and shake the pan to mix. Do not stir with a spoon. Cover the pan and cook for a few minutes. Serve sprinkled with fresh coriander leaves.

Aubergine in coconut milk: Brinjal molee
(*Singhalese*)

2 large aubergines
1 teasp. turmeric powder
salt
ghee or oil for frying
1 medium-sized onion, sliced

1 clove garlic, finely chopped
2 green chillies, finely chopped
1 inch fresh ginger, chopped
1 cup thick coconut milk

Peel the aubergines and cut them into fairly thin slices. Sprinkle with salt and rub on both sides with powdered turmeric. Heat the ghee or oil in a frying-pan and fry the slices on both sides, but do not brown. Remove from the pan and drain. Add a little more fat to the pan and put in the onion, garlic, chillies and ginger. Fry for 5–7 minutes, or until the onion is cooked but not brown. Add the coconut milk, bring to the boil, add the fried aubergines and a little more salt if necessary. Simmer until the sauce has thickened.

Serve with rice.

Aubergine with mushrooms: Baklazany z grzybami
(*Polish*)

3 medium-sized aubergines
1 oz. butter or cooking fat
1 small onion, chopped
8 oz. sliced mushrooms
salt

pepper
1 egg
1 oz. fresh breadcrumbs
1 tablesp. chopped parsley
1 cup thick cream

Cut the aubergines in half lengthways, scoop out the pulp and chop it. Heat the fat in a pan and sauté lightly the onion. Add aubergine pulp and sliced mushrooms and cook until tender. Season with salt and pepper. Cool then stir in the egg and breadcrumbs. Add the parsley and mix well.

Fill the aubergine cases with this stuffing and place on a greased ovenproof dish. Add 2–3 tablespoons water and put in a pre-heated oven to bake in a moderate heat for 20–30 minutes. When the aubergines are nearly ready, pour the thick cream, seasoned with salt, over the vegetables and bake for a few minutes longer.

Fragrant aubergines: Chiehtze hsiang
(*Chinese*)

2 large aubergines
6 dried mushrooms, soaked in water
4 slices bamboo shoots, diced
3 oz. smoked ham, cut into pieces
1 chicken breast, cooked and diced
1 oz. halved peanuts
1 oz. blanched almonds
1 oz. walnuts
oil for deep frying

For the sauce:
4 tablesp. soya sauce
2 tablesp. sherry
1 teasp. sugar
a pinch ve-tsin (monosodium glutamate)

Peel the aubergines and cut into wedges. Cut wedges diagonally into ½ inch pieces. Heat the oil in a deep frying-pan and when it is smoking drop in the aubergine pieces and fry for 5 minutes. Remove pieces and drain. Pour out all but 1 tablespoon of fat. Into this put the drained mushrooms, bamboo shoots, ham and chicken. Fry for 1 minute and add the aubergine pieces and the sauce. Bring to the boil and serve, garnished with fried nuts.

To make the sauce: Mix all the ingredients together.

Mashed aubergines: Bharta
(*Punjabi*)

2 medium-sized aubergines
1 large onion, finely sliced
3 tablesp. ghee or oil
2 medium-sized tomatoes, chopped

1 teasp. coriander powder
½ teasp. red chilli powder
½ teasp. cumin seed powder
salt

Roast the aubergines over a low heat or under the grill until the skin has blackened and the flesh is soft. Peel and mash the pulp. Heat the ghee or oil in a pan and sauté the onion until it is soft and transparent. Add the tomatoes and fry until they are well cooked and have the consistency of thick marmalade. Add the spices and salt and fry for 1–2 minutes. Add the aubergine. Cook for 5–7 minutes on a low heat, stirring to prevent the mixture from sticking to the pan. Serve with chupatties (*see* Section Seven) or as a side dish with curry.

Bean sprouts and green peppers
(Chinese)

8 oz. bean sprouts or 1 tin   2 tablesp. oil
1 large green pepper, shredded   1 tablesp. wine or sherry
pinch of ve-tsin (monosodium   1 tablesp. soya sauce
   glutamate)

Wash the bean sprouts or drain, if tinned. Heat the oil in a pan and
fry them together with the pepper for 1–2 minutes. Add the rest of the
ingredients and fry for a few minutes longer.

Beetroot purée: Rode bieten schotel
(Dutch)

1 lb. cooked beetroot   salt
½ cup thick, white sauce   knob of butter

Peel and mash the cooked beetroot and put in a pan. Stir in the white
sauce and add salt. Cook slowly over a low heat, stirring frequently.
When the pureé begins to boil, add butter and continue cooking for 1–2
minutes.

Cauliflower with ham
(Serbian)

1 medium-sized cauliflower   pepper
3 oz. cooked ham, cut into small   1 cup cream
   pieces   2 egg yolks
salt

Boil the cauliflower in salted water until nearly done. Remove from
water and divide into pieces. Place the cauliflower in a greased fireproof dish and strew the ham pieces over it.

Beat the egg yolks with the cream, season with salt and pepper and
pour over the cauliflower and ham.

Bake in a moderately hot oven until the top is golden in colour
(about 30 minutes).

Punjabi cauliflower: Phul gobi
(Indian)

1 medium-sized cauliflower   ½ teasp. cumin seed powder
ghee or oil for frying   ½ teasp. coriander powder
1 large onion, chopped   fresh coriander leaves, chopped
½ teasp. fresh ginger, chopped   water
½ teasp. red chilli powder   salt
1 teasp. turmeric powder

Put the cauliflower in a saucepan, sprinkle with salt and add a little water. Cover and leave to simmer until half-cooked. Remove from the pan and put on a dish. Break into pieces.

Heat a little oil or ghee in a frying-pan and sauté the onion and ginger until the onion is golden. Mix all the spices and add these to the pan. Fry for a few minutes, add the cauliflower pieces, which should be very dry, and continue to fry slowly until cauliflower is cooked. Before removing this from the pan, sprinkle with chopped coriander leaves.

Louvain carrots
(Belgian)

1½ lb. carrots	2 teasp. sugar
1 small onion, sliced	salt
2 rashers bacon, diced	water
1 oz. butter	

Peel the carrots and cut into quarters. Put them in a saucepan with the bacon, onion, sugar and butter. Season with salt and cover with water. Bring to the boil, then reduce heat. Cover the pan and simmer until the liquid has almost evaporated. Shake the pan to coat the carrots with the juices.

Carrots in batter: Marchew w ciescie
(Polish)

1 lb. young, thick carrots	2 eggs
3–4 tablesp. milk or cream	salt
4 tablesp. flour	butter for frying

Peel the carrots and cook until tender in boiling salted water. Drain in a colander and dry. Cut each carrot into 2–3 pieces lengthways. Heat some fat in a frying-pan. Dip each piece in batter and fry until puffed up and golden.

To prepare batter: Separate egg yolks and whites. Beat the yolks with milk or cream, gradually adding the flour. Season with salt and mix well. Whip the egg whites until stiff and fold into batter.

Carrots with butter: Marchewka z maslem
(Polish)

1 lb. young carrots	salt
2 oz. butter	chopped parsley
1 tablesp. sugar	

Scrape the carrots, cut into thick slices, sprinkle with salt and put on a dish. Cover with a plate. Leave for 1 hour. Put carrots and their liquid in a saucepan, add butter and simmer slowly with the lid on for 30–40 minutes. Serve sprinkled with chopped parsley.

Stuffed chicory: Gefullte chicorée
(*Swiss*)

4 medium-sized chicory sticks	salt
4 tablesp. boiled rice	pepper
4 tablesp. grated Parmesan or	chopped parsley
Gruyère cheese	1½ oz. butter

Put the chicory in a saucepan of salted water. Boil for 10 minutes. Take out of pan and cut in half lengthways. Take out some of the inside leaves. Chop these and mix with the boiled rice and half the grated cheese. Season with salt and pepper. Mix well and fill the hollowed-out chicory sticks. Place chicory in a buttered ovenproof dish, sprinkle the rest of the cheese on top and dot with butter. Cook in a moderate oven for about 10 minutes or until the cheese has melted. Serve sprinkled with chopped parsley.

French beans: Fassoulia
(*Arabian*)

1 lb. French beans	4 tomatoes, cubed
½ cup peanut oil	6 cloves garlic, crushed
2 onions, cubed	salt
2 green chillies, chopped	water

Cut the French beans into 1-inch pieces. Heat the oil in a pan and fry the onions for a few minutes. Add the beans, salt and water and cover the pan. Simmer on a low heat until water has evaporated. Add the chillies and tomatoes. Continue cooking with the lid on until the tomatoes and beans are cooked. Remove from heat and stir in garlic. Serve hot or cold.

Green peas: Petits pois à la Française
(*French*)

1 lb. shelled green peas	½ small lettuce, cut into small
6–8 shallots	pieces
1½ oz. butter	½ teasp. sugar
water	salt

Melt 1 oz. butter in a heavy pan and put in the peas, shallots, lettuce, sugar and salt. Cover the pan and when the butter begins to sizzle, add enough hot water to cover the peas. Simmer over low heat in covered saucepan, for about 45 minutes or until peas are tender. Before serving, stir in the rest of the butter.

Mixed vegetables: Leipziger allerlei
(German)

1 lb. small potatoes	½ lb. green peas
½ lb. French beans	2 oz. butter
½ lb. young carrots	1 teasp. flour
1 small cauliflower	1 tablesp. dried breadcrumbs
sugar	salt

Peel the potatoes (or scrape if young). Put in a pan of salted water and cook. Peel and dice carrots. Cook in very little water until tender. When nearly ready, remove from the heat, sprinkle with flour, add a pinch of sugar, season with salt, mix well and return to heat. Cook for 5 minutes. Cook peas in salted water and set aside. String the French beans, cut into pieces and cook in salted water to which a pinch of sugar has been added. Boil the cauliflower in salted water till tender. Drain.

Heat some butter in a pan and fry the breadcrumbs.

Place the cauliflower on a hot serving dish and arrange the other vegetables round it. Pour over them butter and fried breadcrumbs. This dish can be garnished with croûtons, which may be used to separate the vegetables as required.

Mixed vegetables: Rassa sabzi
(Gujurati)

1 lb. peeled and cubed potatoes	½ teasp. cumin seed powder
1 lb. green peas	1 teasp. coriander powder
½ lb. French beans, cut into pieces	1 teasp. turmeric powder
	1 teasp. red chilli powder
ghee or oil for frying	½ teasp. sugar
1 large or 2 medium-sized grated onions	salt
	hot water

Heat the ghee or oil in a pan and fry each of the first three vegetables separately. Remove from the pan when nearly cooked. Add a little more fat to the pan, if needed, and fry lightly the onion. Add spices and

M

fry for a few minutes. Add the vegetables. Season with salt, add the sugar and about $\frac{1}{2}$–$\frac{3}{4}$ cup hot water. Cover and simmer till vegetables are completely cooked.

Flamed mushrooms: Champignons Flambés
(French)

12 oz. mushroom caps	2 tablesp. brandy
2 oz. butter	2 tablesp. Madeira
salt and pepper	$\frac{3}{4}$ cup thick cream

Peel the mushroom caps and sprinkle with salt and pepper. Melt the butter in a frying-pan and fry the mushrooms over a fairly high heat for about 5 minutes, or until just cooked. Pour in the brandy and set alight. When the flames have died down, add the Madeira and cook until the liquid is reduced by half. Add the cream and cook until the sauce is thickened. Serve the mushrooms on toast.

Note: This is an effective way of serving mushrooms as a savoury when it is done on a spirit stove at the table.

Mushrooms and potatoes: Zrazy z grzybow
(Polish)

8 oz. mushrooms	salt
6 medium-sized potatoes	pepper
1 small onion, chopped	1 cup sour cream
1 oz. butter	

Wash the mushrooms and slice them. Heat the butter in a pan and sauté the chopped onion until golden. Add the mushrooms and cook, stirring all the time. Remove from the pan when cooked and keep the liquid, if there is any left.

Boil the potatoes in their skins until half-cooked. Cool and peel. Slice fairly thinly. Grease an ovenproof dish. Put a layer of potatoes on the bottom, cover with a layer of mushrooms, sprinkle with salt and pepper. Continue until everything is used up, finishing with a layer of potatoes. Add liquid from mushrooms, if available, to the sour cream and pour over the potatoes. Cook in a moderately hot oven for 20–25 minutes.

Note: This is almost a meal in itself and may be served as a light supper dish.

Mushrooms in sour cream
(*Hungarian*)

1 lb. mushrooms	paprika
1½ oz. butter	1 teasp. chopped parsley
1 small onion, chopped	1 cup sour cream
salt	½ teablesp. flour

Wash, trim and slice the mushrooms. Heat the butter in a pan and sauté the onion until golden. Add the mushrooms and continue frying until they are tender. Season with salt and paprika and add the parsley. Blend the flour with the sour cream and stir into the mushrooms. Bring to the boil and simmer for 2–3 minutes.

Serve with croûtons.

Potato balls curry: Aloo ka kofta
(*Indian*)

For the balls:	*For the curry sauce:*
2 lb. potatoes, unpeeled	1 large onion, chopped
1 large onion, finely chopped	1 teasp. turmeric powder
2 tablesp. fresh, chopped coriander leaves	1 teasp. coriander powder
½ teasp. chilli powder	½ teasp. cumin seed powder
2 tablesp. besan flour (gram flour)	½ teasp. garam masala
salt	1 large tomato or 2 smaller ones
oil or ghee for frying	2 tablesp. oil or ghee for frying

To prepare the balls: Boil the potatoes, peel and mash well. Mix with the chopped onion, chopped coriander leaves, chilli powder, salt and the besan flour. Form into small balls and fry in hot, deep fat until golden brown in colour. Drain the balls and keep warm.

To prepare the curry sauce: Heat 2 tablespoons oil or ghee in a pan and fry a chopped onion, but do not brown it. Add the turmeric powder, coriander powder and the cumin seed powder. Fry for a minute or two, add very little water to make a thick gravy and continue cooking. Add the chopped tomato and the garam masala and cook for 5 minutes longer. When the tomatoes have boiled down to a pulp, add the fried potato koftas, cook for a few minutes and serve.

Potatoes in sour cream: Kartofiel so smetanoy
(Russian)

1 lb. potatoes	salt
1 medium-sized onion, chopped	pepper
1 oz. cooking fat	1 cup sour cream

Peel the potatoes and slice them thinly. Heat the fat in a pan and sauté the chopped onion. Add the potatoes and fry on a low heat, turning the slices frequently. Sprinkle with salt and pepper and add sour cream. Cover the pan and simmer slowly, turning the potatoes at intervals. When nearly done, drain off the liquid and continue cooking until potatoes are tender and light brown.

Potato omelette: Tortilla de patatas
(Spanish)

2 medium-sized potatoes	salt
½ small onion, chopped	pepper
1 tablesp. chopped ham or bacon	oil for frying

Peel the potatoes and slice thinly. Heat the oil in a frying-pan and sauté the chopped onion until golden. Add the sliced potatoes and fry on a very low heat until just soft, but not crisp. Pour off excess fat from pan. Beat the eggs and add to them the ham or bacon. Pour this mixture over the potatoes and onions, season with salt and pepper and cook as for an ordinary omelette, turning it once to cook the other side. Turn out on to a hot plate and serve flat, not rolled.

Potato paprikash: Krumpli paprikás
(Hungarian)

2 lb. potatoes	2 teasp. paprika
2 oz. lard	2–3 tomatoes
1 large onion, chopped	1 green pepper
1 clove garlic, chopped	salt
a few caraway seeds (optional)	water

Peel the potatoes and, if large, cut them into finger-length pieces. Heat the lard in a pan and sauté the chopped onion lightly. Add the garlic, caraway seeds and paprika. Stir and add the potatoes and the tomatoes cut into quarters together with the green pepper (cut lengthways into several pieces). Season with salt and add a little water to the pan. Cover and simmer on a low heat until the potatoes are done. If needed, more water can be added during the cooking.

Potatoes stuffed with cheese: Kartoffelmerenken
(*Swiss*)

12 large potatoes	2 tablesp. chopped chives
8–10 oz. cottage cheese	salt
1 tablesp. sour cream	pepper

Peel the potatoes and put them in a steamer. Place this over a saucepan of boiling water and steam the potatoes till they are cooked, but still firm. Remove from the steamer and cut each potato lengthways leaving the base intact.

Mix the cottage cheese, sour cream, chives, salt and pepper together. Place a little of this mixture in the potato. (It may be necessary to scoop out a little of the potato to do this satisfactorily.)

Potatoes with cheese: Pomme de terre au fromage
(*French*)

6 large potatoes	pepper
1 egg yolk	nutmeg
3–4 tablesp. cream	grated Gruyère or Parmesan
butter	cheese
salt	

Wash and scrub the potatoes. Prick each with a fork and bake in a moderate oven until cooked (about 1 hour). Cut a small circular opening on one side with a small spoon. Scoop out the potato pulp, taking care not to break the skin. Mash the pulp in a bowl. Add a lump of butter, egg yolk and cream. Season with salt and pepper and add a pinch of nutmeg. Fill the potato cases with the mixture, sprinkle with cheese, dot with butter and bake in a moderate oven for about 20 minutes, or until golden on top.

Potatoes with ham: Schinkenkartoffeln
(*German*)

2 lb. potatoes	salt
2 oz. butter	pepper
1 large onion, chopped	½ tablesp. flour
6–8 oz. cooked ham, diced	1 cup sour cream

Boil the potatoes in their skins in salted water. When they are half-cooked, remove from the saucepan, peel and slice thickly. Heat 1 oz. butter in a frying-pan and sauté the onion till golden.

Grease an ovenproof dish. Place a layer of potatoes in the dish, sprinkle with some of the fried onion and diced ham. Repeat until all has been used. Cream the other ounce of butter in a bowl and add the flour. Mix well and blend in the sour cream. Pour this mixture over the contents of the ovenproof dish and cook in a hot oven for 30–40 minutes.

Potatoes with onions: Zwiebelkartoffeln
(German)

1½ lb. potatoes	salt
2 medium-sized onions, chopped	pepper
1½ oz. butter	1 cup sour cream
1 tablesp. flour	2 tablesp. grated Gruyère cheese
1 cup hot milk	

Boil the potatoes in their skins in salted water. When cooked, peel and cut into slices. Melt the butter in pan and sauté the onions until golden in colour. Sprinkle the flour over the onions and fry, stirring for a minute, then gradually add the hot milk. Cook for a few minutes until the sauce has thickened. Butter an ovenproof dish and place alternate layers of sliced potato and onion sauce and season each layer with salt and pepper. Finish with a layer of potatoes. Pour the sour cream over the top and sprinkle with grated cheese. Bake in a moderately hot oven for 15–20 minutes, or until the cheese has melted and the potatoes are browned.

Roast flaked potatoes: Zurcher roesti
(Swiss)

1 lb. potatoes	1 oz. butter
2 tablesp. oil	salt

Boil the potatoes in their skins in salted water. When they are beginning to soften but are still waxy (not floury or this recipe will not succeed) take them out of the water and allow to cool. Peel them. Heat the oil and butter in a pan, grate the potatoes on a coarse grater and add to hot oil. Shake the pan over a fairly high heat, then lower temperature, press the potatoes down, sprinkle with salt, cover and cook for 20 minutes, or until a crust has formed at the bottom. Turn the potatoes and brown the other side. The finished dish should be brown and crisp.

Serve with meat or sausages.

Ratatouille niçoise
(*French*)

1½ lb. tomatoes, sliced
1 aubergine, sliced
1 green pepper
1 small marrow, sliced
2 tablesp. olive oil

1 Spanish onion, sliced
1 clove garlic, chopped
bouquet garni
salt
pepper

Skin the tomatoes and cut the green pepper into pieces. Heat the oil in a pan and sauté the onion for a few minutes, add the garlic. Stir once or twice and add all the remaining vegetables and the bouquet garni. Season with salt and pepper. Cover the pan and simmer gently for 1 hour. Remove the lid and allow the mixture to become quite thick. Serve hot or cold.

Red cabbage: Czerwona kapusta
(*Polish*)

1 lb. shredded red cabbage
1 oz. lard
3 tablesp. lemon juice

2 tablesp. sugar
2 teasp. salt
a pinch of cloves

Parboil the shredded cabbage in a saucepan of water. Drain and sprinkle with lemon juice so that the cabbage will retain its red colour. Melt the lard in a pan and put the cabbage in it. Season with salt, add the sugar and a pinch of cloves. Cover the pan and simmer slowly for about 30 minutes, or until the cabbage is soft. Add a little water if necessary during the cooking. Also add more lemon juice or sugar to taste.

Serve with roast duck, goose or pork.

Sauerkraut with beans: Weisse Bohnen mit Sauerkraut
(*Swiss*)

1½ lb. sauerkraut
½ lb. haricot beans
½ lb. streaky bacon, diced
1 oz. lard

1 large onion, chopped
2 cups stock or water
salt

Soak the beans overnight in water. Drain. Melt the lard in a pan and sauté the onion until transparent, add diced bacon and fry for 1–2 minutes. Add sauerkraut, beans and stock or water. Season with salt, cover the pan and simmer for 1–1½ hours.

Serve with sausages and boiled potatoes.

Sauerkraut with salted cucumbers: Kislaya Kapusta s ogurcami
(*Russian*)

1 lb. sauerkraut	pepper
3 salted cucumbers, sliced	1 cup stock
1 oz. lard	3 tablesp. sour cream
½ onion, chopped	½ teasp. sugar
salt	2 teasp. flour

Put the sauerkraut and sliced cucumbers in a bowl and mix well. Melt the lard in a pan and sauté the onion for 1–2 minutes. Add the sauerkraut and cucumbers. Season with salt and pepper and pour in stock. Stir. Cover the pan and simmer on a low heat until the cabbage and the cucumbers are cooked.

Blend the flour with the sour cream and stir into the sauerkraut, together with the sugar. Cook for 5 minutes and serve.

Sauerkraut
(*German*)

2 lb. sauerkraut	1 large onion, chopped
1 oz. lard	salt
1 oz. flour	water

Put the cabbage in a large pan. Cover with hot water and bring to the boil. (If cabbage is too sour, rinse in cold water before cooking.) Cook gently for about 1 hour.

Heat the lard in a frying-pan and sauté the onion lightly, add the flour and fry for a few minutes. Blend in sufficient water to make a roux and bring to the boil. Add this roux to the cabbage and its liquid and season with salt. Stir until the liquid has thickened.

Serve with roast pork, sausages or boiled bacon.

Note: A few rashers of bacon improve the sauerkraut. Dice the bacon and put it in to cook with the cabbage.

Stuffed savoy cabbage
(*Moravian*)

1 savoy cabbage, medium-sized, not too compact	salt
	pepper
6 oz. rice	1 oz. butter
½ oz. dried mushrooms (soaked in water)	1 oz. flour
1 oz. lard or oil	1 cup vegetable stock and milk, mixed (½ cup of each)
1 small onion, chopped	

Remove all loose, outer leaves and the hard centre of the stump and place the cabbage in a large pan with boiling, salted water. Boil for 5–7 minutes and drain, saving the liquid.

Cook the rice until almost tender and remove from pan. In a separate pan boil the dried mushrooms in the water in which they were soaked. When the mushrooms are tender, remove them from pan and chop fairly coarsely. Reserve the liquid in which the mushrooms were boiled. (There should be about 4 tablespoons of this liquid.)

Heat the lard or oil in a frying-pan and fry the chopped onion until golden in colour, add the onions to the boiled rice together with the chopped mushrooms. Season with salt and pepper and stir in the liquid in which the mushrooms were cooked. Place a little of this stuffing (about 2 teaspoons) between each cabbage leaf, taking care not to break off the leaves from the stem. Press the leaves firmly again to form a whole cabbage and tie with a string.

Place the cabbage in a pan, add the liquid in which the cabbage was cooked, cover the pan and simmer slowly for about 1–1½ hours. Melt 1 oz. butter, add the flour and cook for a few minutes without discolouring. Remove from heat and gradually add the mixture of vegetable stock and milk. Return to the heat and stir until the sauce thickens. Season with salt.

Place the cabbage on a hot serving dish, pour the sauce over it and serve.

Stuffed marrows: Lauki
(*Punjabi*)

For the marrows:
2 young marrows
4 tablesp. ghee or oil
2 onions, chopped
salt
1 inch fresh ginger, chopped
½ teasp. coriander powder
½ teasp. chilli powder
½ teasp. turmeric powder
½ teasp. cumin seed powder
1 teasp. garam masala

For the stuffing:
1 tablesp. ghee or oil
½ onion, chopped
2–3 green chillies, sliced thinly
fresh coriander leaves
8 oz. green peas
panir
salt

For the panir: (Indian cheese)
2 pints milk
sour milk
1 tablesp. vinegar or lemon juice
salt

Peel the marrows and cut off the tops. Use these to make a lid. Scoop out seeds and some of the flesh inside the marrows. Place the marrows in a saucepan of boiling water and cook slowly until half-cooked. Remove from pan. Stuff the marrows with the cheese mixture, put tops on to form lids and secure with toothpicks. Heat 2 tablespoons oil or ghee in the pan and sauté two chopped onions for a few minutes. Add the ginger and spices, season with salt and fry for a few more minutes. Add a little hot water to make a thick gravy and place stuffed marrows in the pan. Cover and simmer until tender.

To prepare the stuffing: Heat 1 tablespoon ghee or oil in a frying-pan and fry lightly ½ an onion, chopped. Add the green chillies, coriander leaves, green peas and the panir. Season with salt and stir.

To prepare the panir: Bring milk to boil and add a little sour milk, vinegar or lemon juice and salt. Remove from heat as soon as the milk curdles. Place a colander over a bowl and put a piece of muslin in the colander. Pour the milk into it and tie the muslin up. Place a lid over the muslin and press it down with a weight. Leave for several hours to allow the water to drain off. Take out the cheese from the cloth. A little complicated, perhaps, but worth the effort.

Gujurati tomatoes
(*Indian*)

1 lb. large firm tomatoes	pinch cinnamon
2 oz. ghee or butter	2–3 tablesp. boiled rice
1 small onion, chopped	1 heaped tablesp. fresh bread-
½ teasp. turmeric powder	crumbs
½ teasp. curry powder	salt

Cut the tops off the tomatoes, scoop out the pulp and drain the tomato cases. Heat the fat in a pan and sauté the onion till golden. Add the turmeric, curry powder, cinnamon, rice and breadcrumbs. Chop the tomato pulp and stir into the rice mixture. Season with salt and cook for a few minutes. Cool slightly, then fill the tomato cases with the mixture. Place the tomatoes, when filled, on a greased oven-proof dish and cook in a hot oven (400° F., Gas reg. 6) for 20–30 minutes.

Serve as a side dish for dinner.

Tomatoes and green peppers: Lecso
(*Hungarian*)

4 medium-sized tomatoes	3 rashers bacon, diced
3 green peppers	salt
1 medium-sized onion, chopped	paprika
1 oz. lard	

Scald the tomatoes in a saucepan of boiling water. Skin them and divide them into quarters. Core the peppers and slice thickly. Melt the fat in a pan and sauté the chopped onion, together with the bacon. When the onion is golden, add the peppers and tomatoes. Season with salt and add paprika. Simmer, covered, until the tomatoes have the consistency of marmalade and the green peppers are tender.

Note: Sliced Hungarian sausage or a continental garlic sausage may be used instead of the bacon.

Transylvanian beans
(*Rumanian*)

1 lb. French beans	paprika
1 oz. butter	1 tablesp. chopped onion
½ oz. flour	1–2 tablesp. wine vinegar
salt	¼ cup sour cream

Choose young beans. String them and cut off the tips. Cut them into diagonal strips. Boil in salted water. Drain when cooked, but retain some of the liquid.

Make a roux with the butter and flour and when lightly brown, add the chopped onion and fry for 1–2 minutes, blend in a little of the water in which the beans were cooked. Add the beans and bring to boil. Season with salt and add a little paprika. Add the vinegar and simmer for a while. Before serving add the sour cream.

SALADS

Aubergine salad: Brinjal salad
(*Indian*)

2–3 medium-sized aubergines	1 heaped teasp. sugar
1 large onion, sliced	1 tablesp. salad oil
1 tablesp. coriander leaves, chopped	1 tablesp. wine vinegar
2–3 green chillies, chopped	salt

Bake the aubergines in the oven or under the grill until the skins are
blistered and nearly black. Scoop out the pulp and place in a bowl.
Add the finely sliced onion, coriander leaves, chillies, sugar, salad oil
and vinegar and mix well. Keep in a cool place for several hours before
serving.

Aubergine salad: Salata de vinete
(*Rumanian*)

2 aubergines	3 tablesp. olive oil
½ onion, grated	lemon juice or wine vinegar to taste
salt	
pepper	

Bake the aubergines as described above. Peel and mash the pulp. Put
in a bowl and add the grated onion, salt and pepper. Gradually add
the olive oil, blend well and stir in the lemon juice or vinegar. Chill
before serving.

Bean salad: Salade des haricots verts
(*French*)

1 lb. French beans	2 tablesp. wine vinegar or lemon juice
3 medium-sized tomatoes	3 tablesp. salad oil
1 spring onion	1 tablesp. cream
salt	1 teasp. chopped tarragon
pepper	

String the beans and cook them in a saucepan of boiling, salted water (uncovered) for 15–20 minutes. Drain and put in a salad bowl. Slice the tomatoes thinly and cut up the spring onion into small pieces. Put these in a bowl and add salt, pepper, vinegar or lemon juice and the oil. Leave for 30 minutes or 1 hour, then pour half the juice over the beans and mix well. Place the tomato slices and onion on top of the beans. Add the cream and tarragon to the rest of the tomato juice. Mix well and pour over the bean salad in the bowl.

Celeriac salad: Salade de celeri-rave
(*French*)

2 celeriacs	2 tablesp. olive oil
1 tablesp. lemon juice	1 dessertsp. French mustard
salt	3 tablesp. cream
a pinch sugar	

Peel and wash the celeriacs and cut them into pieces about the size of a matchstick. Sprinkle with salt and lemon juice to keep them white and put on one side.

Mix the olive oil with the mustard in a bowl. Add the sugar and stir in the cream. Blend well and pour over the celeriac. Mix and leave for 1–2 hours before serving.

Cheese salad: Käsesalat
(*German*)

6 oz. Gruyère cheese	½ teasp. chopped dill
¼ lb. potatoes, boiled in skins	3–4 tablesp. mayonnaise
4 hard-boiled eggs, sliced	salt
½ small onion, finely chopped	pepper

Cut the cheese into small cubes. Peel the potatoes and slice thinly. Arrange the potatoes, cheese and sliced eggs in a bowl. Mix with chopped onion and dill and season with salt and pepper. Pour over mayonnaise and blend this into the mixture.

Cucumber salad
(*Danish*)

1 cucumber	1 tablesp. sugar
1½ teasp. salt	2 tablesp. salad oil
2 tablesp. water	2 tablesp. wine vinegar

Slice the cucumber very thinly. Put on a plate and sprinkle with salt. Press the cucumbers down by putting another plate on top and a weight on top of the second plate. Leave for 30 minutes. Strain and if too salty rinse in cold water. Dissolve the sugar in a bowl with 2 tablespoons water. Add the vinegar and stir in the salad oil. Place cucumber in a serving dish. Add dressing.

Serve with grilled chicken.

Fish salad: Basler Fischsaalat
(*Swiss*)

1 lb. boiled, white fish	a few capers
2 hard-boiled eggs	1 tablesp. olive oil
2 gherkins	1 tablesp. lemon juice
salt	2 tablesp. mayonnaise
3 anchovy fillets	

Either flake fish or cut into pieces and put in a bowl. Cut the eggs and gherkins into small cubes and add to the fish together with the chopped anchovies and capers. Add the oil and lemon juice and stir in mayonnaise. Mix well and serve on a bed of lettuce leaves. Garnish with olives.

Green pepper salad: Insalata di pepperoni
(*Italian*)

2 large green peppers	sprig fresh basil, chopped or
4 large tomatoes	½ teasp. dried basil
4 spring onions	2 tablesp. olive oil
½ teasp. salt	2 tablesp. wine vinegar or lemon
½ teasp. freshly ground black pepper	juice

Core the peppers and remove the seeds and pith. Cut them into thin slices. Cut the tomatoes into thin slices. Chop the onions. Arrange them on a dish and pour over the dressing made from the vinegar, oil, herbs and seasoning mixed together.

Herring and potato salad
(*German*)

2 salted herrings	capers
4 potatoes	mayonnaise
salt	pickled mushrooms
pepper	gherkins

Soak the salted herrings in water for at least 18 hours. Remove bones and cut into small pieces. Boil the potatoes in salted water, allow to cool before peeling and slicing them. On a round serving dish place a layer of potatoes, cover with a layer of herrings, sprinkle with salt and pepper and add a few capers. Continue until all potatoes and herrings have been used up, forming a small pyramid on the plate. Cover the top and sides with thick mayonnaise and garnish with gherkins and pickled mushrooms.

Mixed salad: Gado-gado
(*Indonesian*)

6 oz. cabbage, shredded	*For the sauce:*
8 oz. bean sprouts	16 red chillies, seeded and ground
4 oz. French beans, cut into 1-inch lengths	or
	1 tablesp. chilli powder
2 large potatoes	½ lb. roasted peanuts
2 hard-boiled eggs	1½ cups coconut milk
3 spring onions, cut into small pieces	2–3 tablesp. sugar
	2–3 tablesp. lemon juice
1 large cucumber or 2 small ones, sliced	salt

Parboil the shredded cabbage in water. Scald the bean sprouts. Cook the beans in salted water and drain when cooked. Cook the potatoes in salted water. Drain, peel and slice when cooked. Place these vegetables with the eggs, onions and cucumber in a large bowl or on a platter and serve the sauce separately.

To prepare the sauce: Grind or pound the peanuts with the chillies. Mix with the lemon juice, sugar and coconut milk. Put this in a saucepan and bring to the boil. Simmer for a few minutes, adding more sugar and lemon juice to taste, if required.

Onion salad with curd: Dhai cachumber
(*Pakistani*)

3 onions, very finely sliced	½ inch fresh ginger, chopped finely
1 teasp. salt	
1 large tomato, chopped	1 dessertsp. chopped fresh coriander leaves
½ lb. curd or yoghurt	
4–5 green chillies, chopped	

Place onions in a bowl and sprinkle with salt. Leave for 30 minutes. Drain and toss on kitchen paper to absorb moisture. Put onions in a serving bowl, add the chopped tomatoes, chillies, ginger and coriander leaves and stir in the curd or yoghurt. Serve very cold.

Red cabbage salad: Salata z czerwonej kapusty
(*Polish*)

1 lb. red cabbage	½ teasp. sugar
2–3 tablesp. olive oil	chives
salt	lettuce
2–3 tablesp. lemon juice or wine vinegar	

Shred the cabbage thinly, scald in boiling water and drain. Rinse with cold water and allow to cool in a colander.

Mix the salad oil in a bowl with the vinegar or lemon juice. Add the salt and sugar.

Put the cabbage on a serving dish and pour the dressing over it. Mix well. Sprinkle the top with chives and put lettuce leaves around the cabbage to decorate it.

Spinach with yoghurt: Esfenaj-va-mast
(*Persian*)

1 lb. spinach	8 oz. yoghurt
1 teasp. salt	¼ teasp. black pepper

Wash the spinach well and cut off the stems. Put in a saucepan with salt and a very little water and cook until tender. Drain and chop finely. Place chopped spinach in a serving bowl and mix in the yoghurt and pepper.

SECTION TEN

Desserts

Cold desserts

Almonds with sugar (*Persian*)
Baked apple compote (*German*)
Biscuit tortoni (*Italian*)
Brandy cream (*French*)
Chestnut gâteau (*Belgian*)
Chocolate cream (*Austrian*)
Coconut custard (*Malaysian*)
Crême clermont (*French*)
Diplomate aux confitures
  (*French*)
Fruit jelly (*Russian*)
Fruit jelly with cream (*Danish*)
Ice cream (*Indian*)
Iraqi pudding (*Iraqi*)
Maltese rice (*Maltese*)
Melon surprise (*French*)
Orange halva (*Persian*)
Pascha (*Russian*)
Pears cooked in wine (*French*)
Rasghulla (*Bengali*)
Rice cake (*German*)
Semolina mousse (*Swiss*)
Sweet yellow rice (*Pakistani*)
Soufflé Riviera (*French*)
Toffee apples (*Chinese*)
Whipped sour cream (*German*)

Hot desserts

Apple charlotte (*Swiss*)
Apples en belle-vue (*French*)
Apple soufflé (*German*)
Apricot dream (*Austrian*)
Banana balls (*Indian*)
Carrot halva (*Indian*)
Cheese omelettes (*Italian*)
Cheese pancakes (*Russian*)
Coconut dumplings (*Parsee*)
Emperor's omelette (*Austrian*)
Flaming pancakes (*French*)
Hungarian pancake gâteau
  (*Hungarian*)
Lamb's tails (*Chinese*)
Plum dumplings
  (*Czechoslovakian*)
Rice pudding (*Punjabi*)
Rice soufflé (*Belgian*)
Sour cream pudding
  (*Czechoslovakian*)
Sour milk pancakes (*Polish*)
Vermicelli (*Pakistani*)
Viennese soufflé (*Austrian*)
Viennese nockerl (*Austrian*)

N

COLD DESSERTS

Almonds with sugar: Baghlava Khame Zafar
(Persian)

1 lb. almonds, blanched and shredded	3 egg whites
1 lb. icing sugar	1½ tablesp. castor sugar
rose water	2 tablesp. pistachio nuts, chopped

Mix the shredded almonds with the icing sugar and add enough rose water to make a paste. Rinse a square baking tin with cold water and spread the paste evenly in the tin.

Whip the egg whites until stiff and fold in the castor sugar. Spread the meringue over the almond paste in the tin and leave it to set for about 1 hour. When firm cut into squares and sprinkle with chopped pistachio nuts.

Baked apple compote: Gebackenes Apfelkompott
(German)

2 lb. cooking apples	2–3 tablesp. apricot jam
6 oz. sugar, or to taste	2 egg whites
¼ cup white wine	3 tablesp. sugar
small stick cinnamon	jam for decoration

Peel, core and quarter the apples. Place them in a saucepan, add the sugar, wine and cinnamon. Cover the saucepan and cook until the apples are reduced to a pulp. Remove the lid and continue cooking for a while until the apples have the consistency of marmalade. Remove cinnamon. Transfer apples to an ovenproof dish, smooth the top with a knife and spread the apricot jam over the apple pulp. Whip the egg whites until stiff and fold in sugar. Cover the apples and apricot jam with the meringue and bake in a slow oven until the meringue is set and lightly coloured. Remove from the oven. Cool. Serve cold and garnish the meringue with blobs of jam.

Biscuit tortoni
(*Italian*)

2 cups double cream	¾ cup crushed macaroons
4 oz. icing sugar	½ cup chopped walnuts
2 egg whites	1 tablesp. sherry or rum

Whip the cream in a bowl and gradually add the sugar. Beat the egg whites until stiff in another bowl and fold into the cream mixture. Add the macaroons and walnuts. Finally add the sherry or rum. Pour the mixture into individual paper cases and freeze in the freezing compartment of the refrigerator.

Brandy cream: Crême au cognac
(*French*)

6 eggs	1 teasp. vanilla essence
4 oz. castor sugar	2 tablesp. brandy
8 oz. thick cream	1 tablesp. hot water
1 tablesp. gelatine	

Separate the eggs. Beat the yolks with the sugar until they are thick and pale in colour. Soak the gelatine in a little cold water and dissolve in a tablespoon hot water and cool. Add to the beaten egg yolks and mix well. Beat the cream till stiff and stir into the egg mixture. Whip the egg whites and fold them in. Add the vanilla essence and the brandy. Tie a band of oiled paper round the outside of a soufflé dish, so that it is 3 inches higher than the dish. Pour in the mixture to come 2 inches above the edge of the dish. Place in the refrigerator to set. When set, remove the paper and decorate the top with chocolate shavings or glacé cherries.

Chestnut gâteau: Gâteau aux marrons
(*Belgian*)

1 tin unsweetened chestnut purée (approx. 16 oz.)	2 tablesp. Cointreau or any other liqueur
3 tablesp. icing sugar	8 oz. choclate for icing
2 oz. margarine or butter	whipped cream
4 oz. plain chocolate	

Put the chestnut purée in a bowl and add the sugar. Cream the softened butter, melt the chocolate and mix them with the chestnut purée. Add the liqueur and beat the mixture until well blended. Use an electric mixer if available. Leave in a cold place for several hours or overnight. Form into a thick roll and place on a dish or press into a greased loaf tin and when set (after several hours), turn out and coat with chocolate icing.

Slice thinly and serve with whipped cream.

Chocolate cream: Schokoladencreme
(Austrian)

4 oz. chocolate	3 eggs
1–2 tablesp. water	1 tablesp. rum or brandy
1 tablesp. sugar	½ cup cream

Put the chocolate, water and sugar in a bowl, in a double boiler or over a pan of hot water until chocolate is melted and mixture creamy. Cool. Separate the egg yolks from the whites. Beat the yolks and add to the chocolate mixture. Stir in the rum or brandy. Whip the cream and stir it in. Whip the egg whites stiffly and fold them in. Pour the cream into a glass bowl or into individual glasses. Decorate with whipped cream and glacé cherries.

Coconut custard: Sarikauja
(Malaysian)

1 large coconut	4 oz. sugar
4 eggs	few drops essence of rose water

Scrape the coconut and place the flakes in a bowl. Pour ½ cup water over them and leave for 10 minutes. Transfer the flakes to a muslin bag or a colander and press the milk from the flakes. It should make two cups. If there is not sufficient, add more water to the flakes and press again. Beat the eggs and the sugar until light and creamy. Add the coconut milk and rose water and mix well together. Pour into a greased mould, cover with greased paper and steam over a saucepan of hot water for about 1 hour. Serve chilled.

Crème clermont
(French)

3 eggs	1 oz. gelatine
2 oz. sugar	½ pint whipped thick cream
1 pint milk	marrons glacés for decoration
12 oz. chestnuts	1 tablesp. hot water
3 tablesp. rum or brandy	

Lightly beat the eggs with the sugar. Bring the milk to the boil, and gradually pour it over the beaten eggs, stirring all the time. Return the mixture to the pan and stir over a low heat until it thickens and will coat the back of a spoon.

Slit the chestnuts and cook them in boiling water for 20 minutes. Drain, remove the skins and pass them through a sieve. Stir the chestnut purée and the rum or brandy into the custard. Add the gelatine, which has been dissolved in a tablespoon hot water. Allow the mixture to cool. When it begins to thicken, fold in about three-quarters of the whipped cream. Rinse a mould in cold water and pour in mixture. Leave in a cool place to set. When set, unmould and decorate with marron glacés and the rest of the cream.

Diplomate aux confitures
(French)

14 oz. sponge fingers	5 egg yolks
1 lb. apricots or peaches, fresh or	5 oz. sugar
tinned	1 pint milk
apricot or raspberry jam	vanilla pod or essence
rum or kirsch	sweetened water

Dilute the rum or kirsch with sweetened water. Moisten the sponge fingers and arrange them on the bottom and around the sides of a round cake tin. Spread jam on the bottom layer. Drain fruit (if tinned) and place some on the jam. Add a layer of sponge fingers. Continue until the fruit, jam and sponge fingers have been used up, finishing with a layer of fingers. Press down lightly and leave in a cold place for several hours, or overnight.

Cream the egg yolks with the sugar. Boil the milk (with the vanilla pod, if used), and add to the egg yolk mixture. Cook over a pan of hot (not boiling) water, stirring until the custard thickens and coats the back of a spoon. Do not overcook or it will curdle. Remove from the heat and cool. Leave vanilla pod in bowl or add vanilla essence.

Turn out the cake on to a serving dish and cover with the custard (having first removed the vanilla pod). Serve well chilled.

Fruit jelly: Kisiel
(Russian)

1 lb. raspberries	1 cup water
3 oz. sugar	2 tablesp. cornflour

Place the raspberries in a muslin bag and add a little water. Squeeze this over a bowl to get 1 cup juice. (If this does not produce enough juice, add more water to raspberries and squeeze again.) Boil the water and sugar and add the juice. Blend the cornflour with a little water to make a paste and add this slowly to the boiling juice, stirring to avoid lumps. Cook until the mixture thickens. Add more sugar if required. Pour the mixture into a rinsed serving bowl or mould and cool. Serve with cream.

Fruit jelly with cream: Rodgrod med flode
(Danish)

1 lb. fruit	4 tablesp. sweet white wine
1 pint water	vanilla essence
8 oz. sugar	whipped cream
1½ oz. cornflour	castor sugar

Put the washed fruit in a saucepan, add water and bring slowly to the boil. Cook for 10 minutes and remove from the heat. Pass through a sieve and return the juice to the pan with the sugar and the vanilla. Bring to the boil. Blend the cornflour with the wine and stir into the juice. Simmer until thickened. Pour into individual glasses and sprinkle with castor sugar. Cool and decorate with whipped cream.
Note: The best fruit to use is either red currants or a mixture of raspberries, red currants and cherries. The jelly can also be made with frozen fruit when the fresh fruit is out of season.

Ice cream: Kulfi
(Indian)

2 pints milk	1 oz. shredded pistachio nuts
2 tablesp. sugar	a little green colouring
1 oz. shredded almonds	½ teasp. powdered cardamoms

Simmer milk on a very low heat until it is reduced to 1 pint. Add the sugar and stir in the nuts and cardamoms. Mix well and add a drop of green colouring. Pour the mixture into a 'kulfi' or any other mould. Cover and leave to freeze for 3–4 hours.
Note: A 'kulfi' is a mould in the shape of a cornucopia and has a lid, but any mould will do. To make ice cream of a richer consistency reduce the milk to ¾ pint during simmering and add ¼ pint double cream.

Iraqi pudding
(*Iraqi*)

8 oz. sugar	2 oz. semolina
1 cup water	2 oz. blanched and chopped
⅓ cup oil	almonds
6 oz. flour	

Boil the sugar and water in a pan to make a syrup. Heat the oil in another pan and gradually add the flour and semolina. Keep stirring to avoid lumps. Cook until the paste becomes light brown in colour. Remove from heat and add the chopped almonds and the syrup. Mix well and return to the heat for 1–2 minutes, until the mixture is thick. Pour on to a greased flat dish and cut into squares before it cools. Serve cold.

Maltese rice
(*Maltese*)

8 oz. long grain rice	2 oranges
2 cups sweet white wine	peaches or apricots in thick syrup
8 oz. sugar	3–4 teasp. brandy or Maraschino

Cook the rice in a large saucepan. Add water, bring to the boil and cook fairly fast, until the rice is half-cooked (about 10 minutes). Drain. Pour the wine into a saucepan, add the sugar, the juice of 2 oranges and the grated rind of 1 orange. Stir well and bring to the boil. Add the drained rice, lower the heat and simmer very slowly until the rice is soft. When ready the rice will be thick and of a syrupy consistency.

Rinse a mould with cold water and sprinkle with sugar. Place a layer of cooked rice on the bottom and cover with the drained fruit retaining the syrup. Place the rest of the rice on the fruit and leave for several hours in the refrigerator to set. Turn out on to a serving dish and pour over the fruit syrup mixed with brandy or Maraschino.

Melon surprise
(*French*)

1 large melon	cherries, peaches, apricots, grapes
castor sugar to taste	(or any fruit in season)
2–3 tablesp. liqueur or sweet	
white wine	

Cut the top off the melon, remove the pips and cut out the pulp, leaving the melon shell. Cube the melon pulp and mix with the fruit (tinned fruit may also be used). Add castor sugar to taste and stir in the liqueur or wine. Mix well and fill the melon shell with the fruit mixture. Put back the top of the melon. Keep in a cold place until ready to serve.

Orange halva: Halva pourtaghal
(*Persian*)

6 oz. butter	1 cup water
8 oz. rice flour	saffron
grated rind of 2 oranges	chopped pistachio nuts
8 oz. sugar	

Heat the butter in a saucepan and slowly add the rice flour, stirring continuously. Add the orange rind and cook until the mixture turns light brown in colour, stirring all the time. In a separate saucepan, dissolve the sugar in water and add a pinch of saffron. Stir the syrup into the flour mixture and cook until the fat separates from the flour and the mixture is thick. Turn on to a greased plate, smooth the surface and sprinkle with pistachio nuts. Serve cold.

Pascha
(*Russian*)

A sweet made with curd cheese which is traditionally served at Russian Orthodox Easter.

2 lb. curd cheese	5 oz. sultanas
6 oz. butter	3 oz. blanched almonds, chopped
6 oz. castor sugar	1 teasp. vanilla
¾ cup sour cream	grated rind of 1 lemon

Beat the cheese until smooth and add the butter, creamed with sugar. Stir in the cream and the remaining ingredients and mix well.

Line a perforated mould or dish with muslin and put the curd mixture in it. Press down with a weight to allow the mixture to drain and leave in a cold place for several hours or overnight.

Turn out on a serving dish, carefully remove the cloth and decorate with preserved fruits and nuts.

Note: The mould should traditionally be of a pyramid shape.

Pears cooked in wine: Compote de poires au vin
(*French*)

6 pears	½ cup red wine
2 oz. sugar	glacé cherries
1 small stick cinnamon	1 cup water

Peel the pears, leaving them whole. Do not remove the stalks. Put the sugar in a saucepan, add the wine, cinnamon and water. Bring to the boil. When the syrup is boiling, place the pears in it and cook gently for about 45 minutes, or until tender. Remove the pears, place on a serving dish, standing upright and place a cherry around the stem. Boil the syrup to thicken and pour it over the pears.

Rasghulla
(*Bengali*)

4 cups milk	1 cup sugar
juice of 2 lemons	1 cup water
1 tablesp. flour	

Heat the milk in a saucepan and add the lemon juice to curdle it. When the milk is completely curdled, remove from the pan and put in muslin over a bowl to drain. When almost dry, put a heavy weight on top to extract all the whey. Add the flour to the curdled milk and knead to a soft dough. Form into small balls the size of a marble. Boil the sugar and water to a syrup and drop the balls into it. Cook on a slow heat for 15 minutes. Serve in the syrup, chilled.

Rice cake: Reiskuchen
(*German*)

4 oz. rice	2 oz. almonds, blanched and
1 oz. butter	chopped
2 pints milk	1 tablesp. rum
small stick cinnamon	jam
4 eggs	dried breadcrumbs
3 oz. sugar	vanilla sugar

Wash the rice, drain and put in a saucepan with the butter, milk and cinnamon. Bring to the boil and simmer until rice is very soft and all the milk is absorbed. Cover the pan during this time. Remove the cinnamon. Pass the rice through a sieve or put it in a liquidizer.

Separate the eggs. Cream yolks with the sugar, add to the rice with the chopped almonds and the rum. Mix well. Whisk the whites stiffly and fold into the rice mixture.

Grease two 7-inch baking tins and sprinkle with dried bread-crumbs. Put the rice mixture in and bake in a moderate pre-heated oven (350° F., Gas reg. 4) for 30–40 minutes. Remove from the tins. Spread one cake with apricot or strawberry jam and cover with the second cake. Sprinkle with vanilla sugar and serve.

Note: This may also be served hot.

Semolina mousse: Griess-kopfli
(*Swiss*)

4 oz. semolina	2 eggs
1¼ pint milk, or milk and water	2–3 tablesp. double cream
2 tablesp. sugar	grated rind of 1 lemon
1 oz. butter	vanilla essence

Bring milk to the boil, add salt and sprinkle the semolina into it, stirring continuously to avoid lumps. Add the sugar and butter and continue cooking on a slow heat until the semolina is thick. When ready remove from the heat, add the lemon rind and vanilla. Stir in the egg yolks, add the cream and fold in the stiffly whipped egg whites. Rinse a mould with cold water and fill with mixture. Leave in a cold place for several hours to set. Serve garnished with preserved fruit and whipped cream.

Sweet yellow rice: Zarda
(*Pakistani*)

½ lb. long grain rice	4 small cardamoms
saffron	1 tablesp. seedless raisins
4 oz. ghee or butter	4 cloves
6 oz. sugar	1 tablesp. blanched almonds
water	1 tablesp. pistachio nuts

Wash the rice and boil in plenty of water until half-cooked. Add the saffron and mix well. Heat the ghee or butter in a separate saucepan and add the sugar. Stir until sugar has melted, add the cardamoms and cloves. Stir, add the rice, raisins, almonds, and pistachio nuts. Cook on a very slow heat until the rice is done and all the liquid is absorbed. Serve cold with cream or curd.

Soufflé Riviera
(*French*)

2 teasp. gelatine	6 oz. sugar
4 tablesp. water	grated rind of 2 lemons
2 tablesp. lemon juice	chopped almonds
6 egg whites	caramel sauce

Put the gelatine in a small saucepan, add the water and lemon juice and stir over a low heat until dissolved. Beat the egg whites, adding the sugar gradually, until they are very stiff. Add the grated lemon rind and fold in the melted gelatine. Tie a band of oiled paper around the outside of a soufflé dish, 7 inches in diameter. The band should be 2 inches above the rim of the dish. Fill the dish with the mixture. It should not quite reach the top of the paper. Leave in a cold place to set. Serve after the paper has been removed, sprinkled with roasted chopped almonds and serve the caramel sauce (*see* note) separately.

Note: To make caramel sauce you will need 1 cup sugar, 1 cup water, 1 cup cream, vanilla essence. Put the sugar in a heavy pan and stir over a low heat until it has melted and turned dark brown. Slowly add the cup of boiling water and continue cooking until the syrup is the consistency of honey. Cool and stir in the cream and vanilla.

Toffee apples
(*Chinese*)

3 medium-sized apples	⅔ cup sugar
3 tablesp. flour	⅓ cup water
1 tablesp. cornflour	1 tablesp. oil
1 egg white	sesame seeds
oil for deep frying	

Peel and core the apples, then cut each into 6 pieces. Mix the flour with the cornflour and lightly beaten egg white. Add sufficient water to make a thick batter. Put the apples in the batter and turn until well-coated.

Heat oil in a deep frying-pan and fry apples until golden brown. Remove from oil and drain.

Boil the water and sugar in a saucepan to form a syrup and when thick add 1 tablespoon oil. Continue to stir the mixture until a small amount, dropped from the tip of a spoon, forms a thread and becomes golden brown. Put the fried apples into the syrup, mix well and sprinkle with sesame seeds. Place apples on a greased plate. Before serving, plunge apples into cold water.

Whipped sour cream: Creme von geschlagener saurer Sahne
(German)

4 egg whites
2 tablesp. castor sugar
4 tablesp. thick sour cream

lemon rind or vanilla essence to taste

Whip the egg whites until stiff and gradually add the sugar. Continue beating until the egg whites stand up in peaks. Carefully fold in the sour cream and lemon rind or vanilla. Serve in a glass bowl or individual glasses.

HOT DESSERTS

Apple charlotte: Schweizer Apfelscharlotte
(*Swiss*)

2 lb. cooking apples
4 oz. sugar
1–2 tablesp. sweet white wine
grated rind of ½ lemon

1 long French roll or white bread
(crust removed)
strawberry or raspberry jam
butter

Peel, core and quarter the apples and cook them in a saucepan with the sugar and wine until they become a thick purée. Add the lemon rind. Cut the bread into thin slices. Dip in melted butter. Line a greased ovenproof dish or baking dish with the bread and place the apple on top. Level with a knife and dot with jam. Cover the dish with a layer of bread and bake in a hot oven for 30–40 minutes, or until top is browned well.

Note: This can also be made with black cherries or plums.

Apples en belle-vue
(*French*)

1 lb. apples
1 cup syrup (made from 4 oz.
sugar and a little water)
½ cup milk
2 teasp. flour
2 eggs

1 oz. sugar
vanilla essence
a knob of butter
1 tablesp. brandy
2 slices pineapple
jam

Peel and core the apples. Cook gently in the syrup, taking care that they remain whole. Transfer into an ovenproof dish and set aside.

Separate the eggs. Put the yolks into a bowl, add the sugar and beat them until light and fluffy. Add the flour and a little milk. Blend well and add the rest of the milk and the butter. Put in a saucepan and cook on a low heat until the mixture thickens. Take off the heat. Add the vanilla and the brandy and cool a little. Meanwhile put the egg whites in a bowl and whip them stiffly. Add them to the custard. Cut the pineapple into pieces and stir them in. Fill the apples with this mixture. Put blobs of jam on top and bake in a moderate oven for a few minutes.

Pour a little brandy or rum over the apples and ignite. Decorate the dish with shortbread biscuits, or serve the apples on rings made with shortbread pastry.

Apple soufflé: Apfleschaum
(German)

1 lb. cooking apples	3 oz. sugar
2 egg whites	1 oz. blanched almonds

Peel and core the apples and cook them in a saucepan with a tablespoon of water until soft and the consistency of a very thick purée. Cool. Whip the egg whites stiffly, gradually adding the sugar, then stir into the purée.

Grease an ovenproof plate and arrange the mixture in the shape of a pyramid on it. Slice the almonds and garnish the soufflé. Bake in a slow oven (300° F., Gas reg. 2) for 45–60 minutes.

Apricot dream: Aprikosentraum
(Austrian)

1 lb. apricots poached in syrup,	3 tablesp. castor sugar
or 1 lb. tinned apricots	4 oz. macaroons, crushed
sponge fingers	¼ teasp. almond essence
2 egg whites	½ cup thick cream

Drain the apricots and reserve the syrup. Line a glass serving dish with sponge fingers, moistened with apricot syrup. Whip the egg whites until stiff and fold in the sugar, macaroons, almond essence and the whipped cream. Arrange the cream mixture in the shape of a pyramid over the apricots, and chill for several hours.

Banana balls: Kervai
(Indian)

3 large bananas	4 oz. butter
1 tablesp. cornflour	2 tablesp. castor sugar
1½ oz. blanched, chopped almonds	½ tablesp. poppy seeds
¼ oz. pistachio nuts, blanched and	pinch cardamom powder
chopped	pinch cinnamon powder
1½ oz. sultanas	oil or ghee for deep frying

Peel the bananas. Heat the butter in a pan and fry the bananas lightly. Remove from the pan and put into a bowl. Mash to a smooth pulp. Add the cornflour and mix well. Re-heat the butter in the pan and fry lightly the almonds, pistachio nuts and sultanas to a golden colour. Mix the sugar with the cinnamon and cardamom powder and the poppy seeds. Add to the fried nuts. Mix well. Form the mashed banana into 5–6 balls and make a well in each. Stuff the balls with the nut mixture. Roll to keep the filling inside the pulp. Fry the balls in deep oil or ghee. Serve hot.

Carrot halva: Gajjar ka halva
(*Indian*)

2 lb. carrots	4 oz. sugar
3½ cups milk	1 oz. pistachio nuts, blanched
5 dessertsp. ghee or melted butter	1 oz. blanched almonds

Peel and wash the carrots. Grate them finely on to a dish. Put them in a saucepan, add the milk and cook on a low heat, stirring until all the milk has been absorbed and the carrot pulp is nearly dry. Add the ghee or butter and continue cooking. Cook until the pulp begins to turn light brown and the fat is oozing from it. Add the sugar. Cook for 5 minutes, add the nuts (chopped finely). Mix well, remove from the heat. Serve very hot.

Cheese omelettes: Fritelle di ricotta
(*Italian*)

8 oz. ricotta cheese or another very fine curd cheese	2 eggs
	1 tablesp. rum or brandy
2 tablesp. sugar	2 tablesp. flour
salt	butter for frying
rind of ½ lemon	

Place the cheese in a bowl and mix with the sugar, salt, lemon rind, eggs, rum or brandy. Add the flour and mix well. Heat the butter in a frying-pan and place dessertspoons of the cheese mixture in the hot fat. Fry on both sides until golden in colour and serve sprinkled with sugar.

Cheese pancakes: Tvorozniki
(*Russian*)

1 lb. cottage cheese	rind from 1 lemon, grated
2 eggs	flour
2 oz. butter	vanilla sugar, or cinnamon and
2 oz. sugar	sugar
4 tablesp. cream	

Either sieve or mince the cheese and put it into a bowl. Cream the butter, sugar and eggs together and add the cheese. Mix well and stir in the cream and the lemon rind. Add enough flour to bind the cheese mixture (about 1 oz.) and form the mixture into small pancakes. Dip your hands in the flour as you do this and keep the pancakes on a floured board. Heat the butter in a frying-pan and fry the pancakes on a low heat until well browned. Fry on both sides. (If the pancakes fall apart as they are fried, add more flour to those that remain to be fried, but the less flour used, the better.) Serve them hot, sprinkled with vanilla sugar or sugar and cinnamon.

Coconut dumplings: Khaman ladva
(*Parsee*)

1 coconut	½ teasp. cardamom powder
8 oz. sugar	1 oz. sultanas
2 tablesp. ghee or melted butter	1 oz. blanched and sliced almonds
4 tablesp. water	2½ oz. cornflour
1 teasp. vanilla essence	2½ oz. rice flour
½ teasp. grated nutmeg	

Scrape or grate the coconut and mix with sugar. 1 tablespoon of ghee or butter and 4 tablespoons water. Put in a saucepan and cook over a low heat until the sugar dissolves and the mixture is dry. Remove from the heat, cool a little and stir in the vanilla essence, the spices, sultanas and almonds.

Mix the cornflour, rice flour and 1 tablespoon ghee or butter in a pan. Gradually add a little water, stirring until the mixture becomes thick and smooth. Stir over a low heat until all the water has evaporated and the dough leaves the sides of the pan. Remove from the pan and put on a flat dish. Knead with a little ghee or butter and roll into rounds. On each round place a teaspoonful of the coconut mixture and bring the edges together and seal them firmly. Place the

o

dumplings in a greased steamer. Cover with a damp cloth and steam over hot water till well cooked and firm.

Emperor's omelette: Kaiserschmarren
(Austrian)

½ oz. butter	5 eggs
1 cup milk	4 oz. flour
2 tablesp. sugar	1½ oz. sultanas
salt	vanilla sugar

Melt the butter in a pan. Remove from heat. Separate the egg yolks and the whites. Add the milk, sugar, salt and egg yolks to the butter. Mix well and add the flour gradually, stirring to avoid lumps. Add the sultanas and fold in the egg whites which have been whipped until stiff. Liberally grease a large shallow baking tin, pour in omelette and bake in a fairly hot oven for 20 minutes or until golden on top. Remove from the oven and, using two forks, tear the omelettes into small pieces. Turn onto a dish and sprinkle with vanilla sugar.

Flaming pancakes: Crêpes flambées
(French)

4 oz. flour	4 lumps sugar
2 eggs yolks	1 teasp. water
1 whole egg	knob butter
pinch salt	grated rind of 1 orange
1 dessertsp. castor sugar	1 large liqueur glass Grand-Marnier
1 oz. melted butter	
½ pint milk	2 teasp. brandy
1 tablesp. Grand-Marnier	

Sieve the flour and salt into a bowl and make a hollow in the centre. Break the egg into it. Add the egg yolks, sugar and a little of the cold milk. Mix with a wooden spoon. Beat the rest of the milk gradually into the flour and eggs and when it has all been mixed together add the butter which has already been melted. Beat well and leave for 1 hour. Add the tablespoon of Grand-Marnier just before making the pancakes.

Melt some butter in a frying-pan and pour in enough of the batter to cover the pan thinly. (If batter has thickened while standing, add a little more milk.) Brown pancakes on both sides. Keep warm when cooked.

In a small saucepan heat 1 tablespoon of water with 4 lumps of sugar, a little butter, the orange rind and the liqueur-glass of Grand-Marnier.

Fold the pancakes into four and place on a hot fireproof dish. Add the brandy to the contents of the saucepan, pour over the pancakes and set alight.

Hungarian pancake gâteau: Palacsintá torta
(Hungarian)

12 pancakes (use batter as described in recipe above)	1 oz. sultanas 2 oz. castor sugar
4 oz. ground walnuts 1 oz. castor sugar 1 tablesp. rum 1 tablesp. cream	2 oz. melted butter 2 oz. grated chocolate or 2 oz. cocoa 1 oz. sugar
6 oz. cottage cheese 2 egg yolks rind from 1 lemon	apricot jam 2 egg whites 3 tablesp. sugar

Mix the walnuts in a bowl with the castor sugar, rum and cream. Mix the cottage cheese in another bowl with the egg yolks, lemon rind, sultanas and sugar. In a third bowl cream the butter with the chocolate or cocoa and sugar.

Grease a fireproof tin with butter and place a layer of pancakes in it. Spread with a little of the walnut mixture. Add another layer of pancakes and spread these with some of the cottage cheese mixture. Add another layer of pancakes and spread with the chocolate mixture. Add a fourth layer of pancakes and spread with jam. Repeat this in the same order until all the ingredients have been used up. Bake in a moderate oven 350° F., Gas reg. 4, for 15 minutes. Remove from the oven. Make a meringue with two egg whites and 3 tablespoons of sugar. Put this on top and return to the oven to bake for another 15–20 minutes at 325° F., Gas reg. 3, until the meringue is set.

Lamb's tails: Cha yang wei
(Chinese)

7 tablesp. sugar 2 tablesp. water 1 tablesp. flour 3 egg whites	3 tablesp. cornflour blended with 2½ tablesp. water oil for deep frying

Mix 5 tablespoons sugar, flour and water in a bowl and divide into
5 balls. Whip the egg whites in another bowl until stiff and fold in
the cornflour mixture.

Heat the oil in a deep frying-pan and, holding the balls with chop-
sticks or on a fork, coat them with the whipped egg whites. Drop each
in the boiling oil, lower the heat and fry until they are golden brown.
Place on a serving plate and sprinkle with the remaining 2 tablespoons
sugar. Serve hot.

Plum dumplings: Knedliki ze svestkami
(*Czechoslovakian*)

½ pint milk	2 oz. cottage cheese
½ lb. sifted flour	1 egg yolk
pinch salt	fresh plums (or apricots)
sugar lumps	dried breadcrumbs
cinnamon powder	butter
1 dessertsp. sugar	

Put the milk in a saucepan and bring to the boil. Reduce heat. Sift in
the flour and salt. Stir until smooth, adding the sugar and the cheese
(free of lumps). Continue simmering and stirring until the mixture is
quite smooth and comes away from the sides of the pan. Remove from
the heat and beat in the egg yolk. Turn onto a floured pastry board
and knead into a firm dough, adding more flour if necessary. Roll out
very thinly and cut into rounds about 2 inches in diameter. Stone
the fruit. Put a plum, or an apricot, on each round and put a lump
of sugar dipped in powdered cinnamon into each plum or apricot.
Wrap the dough around the fruit and form a dumpling. Fill a
saucepan with water and bring to the boil. Allow to boil rapidly. Drop
the dumplings into this and cook for 5–7 minutes, according to the
size. Be careful not to overcook them. Take out the dumplings. Drain
and serve rolled in breadcrumbs which have been fried in butter.
Dust with sugar and cinnamon.

Rice pudding: Kheer
(*Punjabi*)

3 tablesp. rice	½ oz. blanched, sliced pistachio
1 teasp. melted ghee or butter	nuts
2 pints milk	1 oz. sultanas
¼ teasp. saffron	½ teasp. cardamom powder
4 oz. sugar	1 oz. almonds, blanched and
	sliced

Melt the butter or ghee in a pan. Add the washed and drained rice and fry lightly for 1–2 minutes. Add the cold milk and bring to the boil, stirring continuously. Lower the heat and simmer the rice until the grains are soft. Add sugar and saffron. The saffron should be soaked for a few minutes in 1 tablespoon of hot milk before being mixed with the rice. Continue simmering the rice until it reaches a creamy consistency. Stir frequently. When the rice is cooked, add the almonds, pistachio nuts and sultanas. Simmer for two minutes and serve hot, sprinkled with cardamom powder.

Note: This dish may also be served cold.

Rice soufflé: Souffle su riz
(*Belgian*)

For the meringue:
4 egg whites
6 oz. sugar

For the filling:
4 oz. rice
1 pint milk
2 tablesp. sugar
grated rind of 1 lemon
1 oz. chopped orange peel
2 eggs
salt

Make a meringue with 2 egg whites and 3 oz. sugar and cover the bottom and sides of a deep ovenproof dish or bowl. Bake in a slow oven (300° F., Gas reg. 2) until the meringue is set. Leave in the oven to cool.

Blanch the rice in boiling water and drain. Put it in a saucepan with the milk, sugar and pinch salt. Cook very slowly on a low heat until the rice is soft and the milk absorbed. Remove from the heat and cool a little. Add the grated lemon rind and orange peel. Separate the eggs. Beat the yolks and whip the whites until stiff. Add the beaten yolks to the mixture and fold in the whites.

Remove from the oven the dish containing the meringue and fill with the rice mixture. Whip the remaining 2 egg whites with the rest of the sugar until they are stiff. Cover the rice with the meringue and return the soufflé to the oven to bake at a low temperature until the meringue on top is set.

Sour cream pudding
(*Czechoslavakian*)

For the pastry:
8 oz. flour
6 oz. butter
1 egg yolk
2 tablesp. castor sugar

For the filling:
3 eggs
3 tablesp. sugar
the rind of ½ lemon
¼ cup sour cream
1½ tablesp. flour

To prepare the pastry: Rub the fat into the flour in a bowl. Add the sugar and the egg yolk and knead into a smooth dough. Roll out fairly thinly. Grease a round cake tin and line it with three-quarters of the pastry. Keep the rest for the lid. Put the filling in the pastry case. Put the pastry 'lid' on top and press edges firmly together. Bake in a pre-heated moderately hot oven (375° F., Gas reg. 5) for 35–40 minutes. Turn out on to a dish and sprinkle with sugar.

To prepare the filling: Separate the egg yolks and the whites. Beat the yolks with the sugar until white and fluffy. Add the grated lemon rind, the sour cream and flour. Whip the egg whites stiffly and fold into the mixture.

Sour milk pancakes: Placki z zsiadlego mleka
(*Polish*)

5 oz. carton plain yoghurt
1 egg
pinch salt

2 tablesp. flour
3 oz. butter for frying

Empty the yoghurt into a bowl, add the egg, a pinch of salt and the flour. Mix well to avoid lumps. Heat the butter in a frying-pan and drop tablespoons of the mixture into the hot fat. Spread it out thinly over the pan. Lower the heat and fry the pancakes on both sides until puffed up and golden, adding more butter if necessary. Serve the pancakes flat, sprinkled with sugar and cinnamon or with some jam on each.

Vermicelli: Savia
(*Pakistani*)

½ lb. roasted vermicelli
2 pints milk
a few cardamoms

sugar to taste
a few pistachio nuts
sultanas

Boil the milk in a saucepan until it is reduced to half the quantity. Add the vermicelli, cardamoms and sugar and cook until the mixture is thickened, but still creamy. Remove from the pan and put on a serving dish. Sprinkle with sultanas and pistachio nuts.

Note: When vermicelli is not roasted, melt a little ghee in a pan, add a few cardamoms and the vermicelli and fry on a low heat until slightly browned. (This dish is always offered at the end of the long Ramadan fast.)

Viennesse soufflé
(*Austrian*)

2 oz. butter	1 extra egg white
2 oz. sifted flour	1 teasp. vanilla
1 cup milk	sponge fingers
2 tablesp. sugar	preserved fruit, drained
5 whole eggs	Kirsch, rum or brandy

Melt the butter in a pan and stir in the flour. Gradually add the warmed milk, stirring constantly. Add the sugar and cook on a low heat for about 3 minutes, or until sauce thickens. Remove from the heat and add the vanilla. Separate the egg yolks from the whites. Beat the egg yolks. When the mixture in the pan is cool, add the yolks and beat well. Whip the egg whites until stiff and fold into the mixture.

Butter a 2-pint soufflé dish and line the sides with sponge fingers moistened with the liqueur. Fill the centre with the soufflé mixture. Put the dish in a pan of hot water and bake in a moderately hot oven (375° F., Gas reg. 5) for about 45 minutes.

Viennese nockerl
(*Austrian*)

4 egg yolks	6 oz. sugar
8 egg whites	vanilla sugar
1 oz. flour	1½ oz. butter

Beat the egg yolks in a bowl until light and creamy, add the sifted flour and a little vanilla. Whip the egg whites until very stiff, adding the sugar gradually. The success of this recipe depends on the stiffness of the egg whites.

Heat butter in an 8-inch pan until it bubbles. Tilt and roll the pan to coat the sides with butter. Quickly fold the whipped egg whites into the mixture and turn it into the pan. Divide it into six parts with a spatula. Put the pan on a low heat just long enough for the underside of the mixture to become coloured. Place pan in a very cool oven (250° F., Gas reg. $\frac{1}{4}$) and bake until the top is golden in colour (about 10 minutes). Dust with vanilla sugar and serve at once.

SECTION ELEVEN

Biscuits and Cakes

Biscuits

Almond slices (*German*)
Biscuits (*Punjabi*)
Chocolate crescents (*Austrian*)
Coconut biscuits (*Malaysian*)

Sesame biscuits (*Chinese*)
Polish shortbread with jam
  (*Polish*)

Cakes

Almond cake (*French*)
Apple cake (*German*)
Apple charlotte (*Austrian*)
Apple crumble (*Swiss*)
Beer cake (*German*)
Brown cakes (*Danish*)
Butter cakes (*Swiss*)
Cake Provençal (*French*)
Cakes with date filling (*Maltese*)
Cheese cake (*Hungarian*)
Chocolate cake (*Czechoslovakian*)
Chrust (*Polish*)
Cream tartlets (*Polish*)
Honey cake (*Israeli*)

Linzer torte (*Austrian*)
Little cream cakes (*Austrian*)
Little stars (*Swedish*)
Macaroons (*Italian*)
Malaya layer cake (*Malaysian*)
Mazurek Czekoladowy (*Polish*)
Pear tart Provençal (*French*)
Sachertorte (*Austrian*)
Schaumtorte (*Austrian*)
Schenkeli (*Swiss*)
Snow balls (*German*)
Tort Mickiewicza (*Polish*)
Walnut cake (*German*)
Zebra Kuchen (*German*)

Cakes with yeast

Almond crescents (*Danish*)
Baba (*Polish*)
Baba with rum (*French*)
Dough wreath (*German*)

Kumas (*Indian*)
Poppy seed cake (*Polish*)
Yeast cakes (*Russian*)

BAKING WITH YEAST

Baking with yeast has an undeserved reputation for being difficult, but it is very simple and requires no special skill. It takes a little time as one has to wait for the dough to rise, but the results are well worth waiting for. One has only to remember that all ingredients for yeast dough must be warm, that yeast to become active must be dissolved in tepid liquid (excessive heat or cold will kill it), and that the dough must be allowed to rise slowly in a warm draught-free place. All cakes should be baked in a pre-heated oven set at the temperature indicated in the recipe.

When fresh yeast is not available, use half the quantity in dried yeast.

BISCUITS

Almond slices: Mandelschnitten
(*German*)

8 oz. butter	2 eggs
8 oz. castor sugar	8 oz. flour
4 oz. shredded almonds	1 egg white
4 oz. chopped almonds	rind of 1 lemon, grated

Cream the butter and 4 oz. of sugar in a bowl until fluffy. Add the lemon rind and the shredded almonds. Beat the eggs and add them to the butter and sugar mixture. Add the sifted flour. Knead into a soft dough and leave for 15 minutes. Roll out on a floured board to the thickness of a penny and cut into small circles and squares. Place on a baking sheet, Smear the tops with slightly beaten egg white and sprinkle with sugar and chopped almonds. Cook in a pre-heated oven (375° F., Gas reg. 5) until light golden in colour.

Biscuits: Khatai
(*Punjabi*)

6 oz. flour	1 cup ghee
4 oz. self-raising flour	pistachio nuts
6 oz. castor sugar	cardamoms
silver leaf	

Mix the flour and sugar in a bowl and add the ghee. Knead into a soft dough and divide it into small balls. Roll out each ball on a floured board to make a thin biscuit. Sprinkle each biscuit with some pistachio nuts and cardamoms, put on a greased baking sheet and cook in a moderate oven for 20–30 minutes. Decorate with silver leaf.

Chocolate crescents: Schokoladenkipferln
(*Austrian*)

5 oz. castor sugar	*For icing:*
1 egg white	6 oz. chocolate
5 oz. unskinned almonds, ground	3 oz. unsalted butter
3 oz. chocolate, grated	
rind of 1 lemon, grated	

Cream the sugar with the egg white in a bowl and add the almonds, chocolate and lemon rind. Mix into a firm paste and form into a long roll about the thickness of a finger. Place the roll on a pastry board dusted with sugar, and cut into pieces about 3 inches long. Form the pieces into crescent shapes, place on a greased baking sheet and cook in a moderate oven (350° F., Gas reg. 4) for 15–20 minutes. Remove from the oven, allow to cool, and ice.

To prepare the icing: Put the chocolate and butter into a bowl. Place the bowl over a saucepan of hot water and stir contents until the chocolate is melted and well-blended with the butter. Use at once.

Coconut biscuits: Banget
(*Malaysian*)

4 oz. flour	¼ cup thick coconut milk
4 oz. sago flour	2 eggs
4 oz. castor sugar	

Sieve the flour into a bowl and set on one side. Mix the sugar and coconut milk in a saucepan and bring to the boil, stirring all the time until the sugar has melted. Cool, add the eggs one at a time, beating the mixture well after each egg has been added. Add this mixture gradually to the flour and mix to a stiff paste. Roll out on a floured board and cut into fancy shapes with pastry cutters. Place the biscuits on a greased baking tin and cook in a moderately hot oven (375° F., Gas reg. 5) for 10–12 minutes.

Sesame biscuits: Jei mar beang
(*Chinese*)

8 oz. flour	1 whole egg
½ teasp. baking powder	1 egg white
4 oz. castor sugar	sesame seeds
6 oz. butter or margarine	

Sift the flour and baking powder into a bowl. Make a hollow in the centre and drop in the egg and sugar. Soften the butter or margarine and add. Mix well and knead into a firm dough. Roll out the dough into a sausage on a floured board. Cut the sausage into small pieces. Roll them into biscuits about 2 inches in diameter. Place on a baking sheet. Brush with egg white and sprinkle with sesame seeds. Cook in a pre-heated oven 375° F., Gas reg. 5 for 15 minutes.

Polish shortbread with jam: Kruche ciastka z marmolada
(Polish)

10 oz. flour	the yolks of 3 hard-boiled eggs
4 oz. butter	jam
3 oz. margarine	vanilla sugar
3 oz. icing sugar	

Sift the flour onto a pastry board, add the butter and chop the butter and flour with a knife. Sieve the egg yolks and add this to the fat and flour together with the icing sugar. Knead quickly into a dough. Cover and leave in a cool place for about 20 minutes. Roll out thinly on a floured board and cut out into circles about 2 inches in diameter. Cut a small hole in the centre of half the circles. Place them all on a greased baking sheet and cook in a pre-heated oven (400° F., Gas reg. 6) until golden. Remove and place on a wire rack to cool. When the biscuits are cold, spread jam on those that do not have holes in them. Cover these with the rest. Press lightly together and sprinkle with vanilla sugar mixed with icing sugar. Put more jam in the centre holes.

CAKES

Almond cake: Gâteau aux amandes
(*French*)

4 oz. chocolate	6 oz. castor sugar
2 tablesp. rum or brandy	6 oz. blanched almonds, shredded
1 tablesp. strong coffee	6 eggs
6 oz. butter	½ pint double cream

Break the chocolate into pieces and put in a saucepan with the rum or brandy and coffee and melt over a low heat, or in the oven. In another saucepan melt the butter, add the sugar and almonds and stir in the melted chocolate. Mix over a low heat until all is well blended and smooth. Remove from the heat and cool. Beat the egg yolks and add them to the cooled mixture. Whip the egg whites stiffly and fold them in. Line and grease two 8-inch tins. Pour half the mixture in each tin and spread it over evenly. Cook in a moderate oven (350° F., Gas reg. 4) for 30–35 minutes. Turn out of the tin. Fill with whipped cream and use whipped cream to decorate the top as well.

Apple cake: Apfeltorte
(*German*)

2½ lb. cooking apples	4 oz. butter
4–5 oz. castor sugar	½ teasp. cinnamon
rind of ½ lemon	½ pint double cream
a few cloves (optional)	2–3 tablesp. water
12 oz. sweet biscuits, crushed	

Peel and core the apples. Cut them up and put them into a saucepan with the sugar, cloves (if used), and the thinly pared lemon rind. Moisten with water. Cover the pan and simmer over a low heat until the apples are soft and pulpy. Remove the lid and take out the lemon rind and cloves. Stir the apples till they have the consistency of thick marmalade. Remove from the heat and cool.

Melt the butter in a pan. Crush the biscuits with a rolling-pin and stir the crumbs into the butter. Add the cinnamon and stir well.

Butter an 8-inch loose-bottomed cake tin and place in it a layer of the crushed biscuit mixture. Press down well. Put half the apple pulp on top. Repeat, finishing with a layer of crumbs. Put the tin in a refrigerator and leave for several hours, or overnight. Take out the cake. Turn it out of the tin and decorate with whipped cream and glacé cherries.

Note: This cake may also be served as a dessert.

Apple charlotte: Apfelscharlotte
(*Austrian*)

10 oz. flour	4 oz. sugar
6 oz. butter	½ teasp. cinnamon
6 oz. castor sugar	1 packet vanilla sugar
2 egg yolks	1 rounded tablesp. icing sugar
pinch salt	for decoration
1½ lb. cooking apples	

Sift the flour and salt into a bowl. Rub in the butter. Add 2 oz. sugar and the egg yolks. Knead into a dough and leave for 30 minutes. Divide the dough into two. Roll out one half so that it will fit into a 7-inch square baking tin. Grease the baking tin and line it with the pastry. Cook in a hot oven (400° F., Gas reg. 6) for 10–15 minutes, until the pastry is half-cooked. Remove from the oven and cool a little.

Peel and core the apples. Grate them on a coarse grater. Put the grated apples into a bowl. Add 4 oz. sugar and the vanilla sugar. Mix well. Put this mixture in the pastry case. Roll out the rest of the pastry and cover the apple mixture with it. Press edges firmly together. Put in the oven and cook for 25–30 minutes at the same temperature as above. Remove from the oven and cool. Sprinkle with icing sugar and cut into squares.

Apple crumble: Apfel Krummelkuchen
(*Swiss*)

6 oz. flour	1 egg yolk
5 oz. castor sugar	3 large cooking apples
4 oz. butter	1 dessertsp. lemon juice
¾ teasp. cinnamon	vanilla sugar

Sift the flour and cinnamon into a bowl. Add the sugar and butter. Knead well, then crumble the dough with the fingers or grate on a very coarse grater. Divide the crumbs in two parts. Grease a 7-inch loose-bottomed cake tin. Put one half of the crumbs into it. Peel, core and thickly slice the apples. Arrange the slices in layers on top of the crumbs, sprinkling each layer of apples with sugar. Sprinkle the top layer with lemon juice. Add the rest of the crumbs. Dot with butter and cook in a pre-heated oven at 375° F., Gas reg. 5, for 40–45 minutes. Remove from the tin and serve sprinkled with vanilla sugar.

Beer cake: Bier Kuchen
(German)

8 oz. flour	½ teasp. cinnamon
¼ teasp. salt	½ cup treacle
½ teasp. baking powder	¾ cup dark beer
¼ teasp. bicarbonate soda	2 oz. butter
pinch nutmeg	4 oz. seedless raisins
pinch powdered cloves	2 oz. chopped walnuts

Sift the flour, salt, baking powder and spices into a bowl. Pour the beer and treacle into a saucepan. Add the butter and bring to the boil. Stir until the butter has melted, add the raisins and remove from the heat. Cool the mixture and gradually add the sifted flour. Add the nuts and mix well.

Grease a long loaf tin with butter. Pour in the cake mixture and cook in a pre-heated oven at 350° F., Gas reg. 4, for 45–60 minutes.

Brown cakes: Brune kager
(Danish)

2 oz. butter	1 teasp. water
2 oz. castor sugar	¼ teasp. bicarbonate soda
1 oz. golden syrup	4 oz. flour
½ oz. blanched almonds, chopped	½ teasp. cinnamon
½ oz. mixed peel, chopped	¼ teasp. powdered cloves

Put the butter, sugar and syrup into a saucepan and heat slowly. When the butter has melted, bring to the boil and remove from heat. Stir in the almonds and mixed peel and leave to cool for about 10 minutes. Melt the bicarbonate of soda in water and sift the flour, cinnamon and cloves. Add all to the butter mixture. Knead into a smooth dough and shape into a roll, 2 inches in diameter. Wrap in foil and leave over-night in a cool place but do not put it in the refrigerator. Butter a baking sheet and cut up the dough into thin slices. Put the slices on the baking sheet and cook in a moderately hot oven (400° F., Gas reg.

6) for 8–10 minutes. Remove with a palette knife and cool on a wire rack.

Butter cakes
(*Swiss*)

8 oz. flour	pinch salt
8 oz. butter	vanilla essence
2 oz. castor sugar	jam

Cream the butter and sugar in a bowl until light and fluffy. Add the vanilla essence. Sift the flour and salt and mix half of it into the creamed butter and sugar. Stir in the rest of the flour and continue mixing for 1–2 minutes. Put twelve paper cases on a baking sheet and pipe the mixture into the cases, using a rose nozzle. Pipe the mixture so that it comes higher up the cases at the sides than in the centre. Cook in a pre-heated oven (400° F., Gas reg. 6) for 15 minutes. Cool and dredge with icing sugar. Fill the centres with jam.

Cake Provençal
(*French*)

10 egg whites	*For icing:*
12 oz. castor sugar	10 oz. icing sugar
12 oz. almonds, blanched and shredded	2 tablesp. water
	1 teasp. vanilla essence
juice of 1 lemon	
8 oz. butter	
2 egg yolks	
8 oz. icing sugar	
4 oz. almonds, shredded (not blanched)	
2 tablesp. rum	

Whip the egg whites in a bowl until very stiff. Gradually add the sugar towards the end of the whipping. Fold in the almonds and lemon juice. Divide mixture into four. Draw circles on a greased grease-proof paper and line shallow 8-inch baking tins with the paper. Put a portion of the meringue mixture on each and spread it out. Bake in a slow oven (300° F., Gas reg. 2) for about 1 hour, or until the meringues are dry. Remove from oven and from the tin. Take paper off the meringues.

Cream the butter in a bowl until light and fluffy and gradually add

P

the egg yolks, beating after each has been added. Slowly add the
sugar and mix well. Stir in the almonds and rum. Spread this cream on
each of the meringue circles and join them together, pressing very
lightly. Ice with vanilla icing.

To prepare the icing: Put the icing sugar in a bowl, add the vanilla
essence and enough water to make a thick icing. Pour the icing over the
cake and smooth the top and sides with a palette knife dipped in hot
water. (If the icing is too thick, add more water.)

Cakes with date filling: Imqaret
(*Maltese*)

12 oz. flour	¼ teasp. cloves, powdered
1 egg yolk	1 oz. orange peel
1 oz. margarine	1 teasp. lemon juice
rose water to mix	fat for frying
12 oz. dates	

In a bowl, rub the fat into the flour, then add the egg yolk and sufficient
rose water to mix to a soft dough. Knead well. Divide the dough in
half and on a floured board roll out each half very thinly into long
wide strips.

Stone the dates and soak them in water for 30 minutes, then put
them through a mincer with the orange peel. Add the cloves and lemon
juice and blend well. Spread the mixture over one strip of pastry and
cover with the second strip. Cut into round or diamond shapes. Press
down the edges well to prevent the filling from falling out.

In a deep frying-pan, heat some fat and fry the cakes until golden
in colour.

Cheese cake: Rakoczy
(*Hungarian*)

6 oz. flour	*For the filling:*
4 oz. butter	1 lb. cottage cheese
1 oz. castor sugar	2 eggs
	4 oz. castor sugar
	grated rind of 1 lemon
	1 teasp. vanilla
	1 cup sour cream

Put the flour on a pastry board. Cut the butter into it with a knife.
Add the sugar and knead into a dough. Roll out. Grease an 8-inch

loose-bottomed cake tin and line it with pastry. Prick the pastry with a fork to prevent it rising. Cook in a pre-heated oven (425° F., Gas reg. 7) for 10–12 minutes. Remove from oven and cool.

Either sieve the cheese or put it through a mincer and beat it until soft and smooth. Beat the eggs with 3 oz. sugar until thick and add to the cheese. Stir in the grated lemon rind and the vanilla and pour the mixture into the cooled pastry in the tin. Bake in oven at 375° F., Gas reg. 5, for 30 minutes. Remove from the oven and pour over it the sour cream mixed with 1 oz. castor sugar. Return to the oven and cook for 10 minutes at 450° F., Gas reg. 8. Remove from oven, cool in tin and then put in the refrigerator before serving.

Chocolate cake: Cokoladovy dort
(*Czechoslovakian*)

4 oz. butter	*For icing:*
4 oz. castor sugar	1 egg yolk
4 egg yolks	1 oz. castor sugar
2 oz. chocolate, grated, or cocoa	2 teasp. cornflour
4 oz. shredded almonds, un-skinned	vanilla
	¼ pint milk
5 egg whites	3 oz. butter
	3 oz. icing sugar
	2 tablesp. strong black coffee
	2 tablesp. rum

Cream the butter and sugar in a bowl until light and fluffy and add the yolks, one by one, beating well all the time. Add the chocolate or cocoa and the almonds and mix well. Fold in the stiffly beaten egg whites. Butter a 7-inch cake tin and fill with the mixture. Cook in a moderate oven (350° F., Gas reg 4) for 40–45 minutes. Turn out on a wire rack and cool. When cold cut through the middle and spread with icing. Sandwich cake together and put some icing on the top.

To prepare the icing: Cream the sugar and egg yolk in a bowl. Blend the cornflour with half the milk and add this to the egg yolk mixture. Bring the rest of the milk to the boil in a saucepan and stir this into the mixture. Add the vanilla essence. Put the bowl over a saucepan of hot water and stir until the mixture thickens. In a separate bowl, cream the rest of the butter and sugar until light and fluffy and, drop by drop, add the black coffee. Mix well, add the cooled custard, a spoonful at a time. Blend well and add the rum.

Chrust
(*Polish*)

8 oz. flour
3 egg yolks
1 oz. melted butter
pinch salt
1 oz. castor sugar

2–3 tablesp. thick cream
1 tablesp. brandy
icing sugar
vanilla sugar
lard or oil for frying

Mix the flour, egg yolks, butter, salt, castor sugar, cream and brandy to a firm dough in a bowl. Knead and divide into 2 or 3 parts. Flour lightly a pastry board and roll out each piece of pastry thinly. Cut each pastry sheet into strips 1 × 5 inches. Make a slit in the centre of each strip and pull one of its ends through the hole. Heat the fat in a deep frying-pan and drop two or three pieces into the fat at a time. Fry quickly on both sides until pale golden. Do not brown them. (To test the temperature of the fat: drop a small piece of the pastry in it and when it floats immediately and changes colour the fat is ready for frying.) Take out the pieces when cooked. Drain them on kitchen paper and sprinkle while hot with icing sugar mixed with vanilla sugar.

Cream tartlets: Babeczki smietankowe
(*Polish*)

10 oz. flour
7 oz. butter
3 oz. castor sugar
2 egg yolks

For cream:
4 egg yolks
4 oz. castor sugar
1 cup cream
½ teasp. vanilla essence
almond essence

Sift the flour on to a pastry board, add the butter and chop the butter and flour with a knife. Add the sifted sugar and egg yolks. Knead quickly into a firm dough. (If necessary, one more egg yolk may be added to make the pastry stick properly.) Cover and leave for 15 minutes. Roll out the pastry on a floured board. Grease the 'babeczki' moulds (these are small moulds similar to fluted rhum-baba moulds). Line the moulds with pastry and cut enough lids so that each mould can be covered. Three-quarters fill the moulds with the cool cream and cover with the lids. Press edges firmly together. Cook in a hot oven

(400° F., Gas reg. 6) for 30 minutes, or until golden in colour. Remove from the oven and turn out, leaving the moulds with the lids at the bottom.

To prepare the cream: Cream the egg yolks and sugar in a bowl until light in colour. Boil the cream and add it, still boiling, to the sugar and egg yolks. Place the bowl over a saucepan of hot water, add the vanilla and cook, stirring until the mixture thickens. Add the almond essence, remove from the heat and cool.

Note: The moulds can be baked blind and filled with various fillings. One of the most popular fillings is wild strawberries mixed with sugar and covered with whipped cream. Another cream, apart from the one given above, which would make a suitable filling is one made with $\frac{1}{2}$ pint cream or milk, 1 oz. sugar, $\frac{1}{2}$ oz. cornflour, 2 egg yolks and vanilla essence. The cornflour is blended in a bowl with a little of the cream or milk. The rest of the milk or cream is heated and the cornflour added to it. Boil the mixture for a minute or two stirring well all the time. The sugar, vanilla essence and beaten egg yolks are then added and the mixture is cooked, without boiling, to thicken.

Honey cake: Lekach
(*Israeli*)

2 eggs	$\frac{1}{4}$ teasp. salt
2 oz. castor sugar	$\frac{3}{4}$ teasp. baking powder
1 tablesp. strong black coffee	$\frac{1}{4}$ teasp. bicarbonate soda
1 tablesp. cocoa	$\frac{1}{2}$ teasp. powdered cloves
2 tablesp. oil	$\frac{1}{2}$ teasp. cinnamon
$\frac{1}{2}$ cup honey, or honey and treacle in equal parts	$\frac{1}{2}$ teasp. cardamom
8 oz. flour	2 oz. chopped walnuts
	2 oz. blanched almonds

Beat the eggs and the sugar in a bowl until light and fluffy. Add the coffee and stir in the cocoa and the oil. Heat the honey in a bowl over a saucepan of hot water. Cool a little. Add to the egg mixture. Sift the flour, salt, baking powder, bicarbonate of soda and spices in a bowl, then gradually add to the honey and eggs. Stir in the chopped walnuts. Mix well. Line and grease a square baking tin (8 × 8 inches) and pour the mixture into it. Smooth the top and decorate with blanched almonds. Cook in a slow oven (300° F., Gas reg. 2) for 45–60 minutes. Leave in the tin to cool.

Linzer Torte
(*Austrian*)

8 oz. butter	8 oz. almonds, shredded
6 oz. castor sugar	8 oz. flour
2 egg yolks	½ teasp. cinnamon
2 tablesp. rum or brandy	¼ teasp. cloves, powdered
rind of 1 lemon, grated	raspberry or strawberry jam

Cream the butter and sugar in a bowl and beat in the egg yolks, one at a time. Add the rum or brandy and lemon rind. Mix well and add the almonds. Sift the flour and spices in a bowl. Add this to the creamed butter and sugar. Roll out the pastry on a floured board (if it is too soft to handle, leave for 30 minutes). Grease an 8-inch round, shallow baking tin and line it with about three-quarters of the pastry. Cut the rest of the pastry into strips. Spread the jam in the pastry case and cover with pastry strips, forming a lattice pattern. Cook in a pre-heated oven at 400° F., Gas reg. 6, for 10 minutes, then reduce the temperature to 350° F., Gas reg. 4, and cook for 20–30 minutes. Before serving the cake, fill the hollows with more jam and cut into wedges.

Little cream cakes: Kleine Sahnekuchen
(*Austrian*)

10 oz. flour	2 egg yolks
5 oz. butter	2–3 teasp. thick cream
4 oz. castor sugar	vanilla essence
1 egg	cinnamon

Put the flour on to a pastry board. Chop the butter into it with a knife. Make a hollow in the centre and drop the egg and egg yolks into it. Add the castor sugar, cream and vanilla essence and knead into a firm dough. Roll out and cut into rounds with a pastry cutter. Brush with melted butter or beaten egg and sprinkle liberally with sugar and cinnamon. Put on a baking sheet and cook in a moderate oven (350° F., Gas reg. 4) for 20 minutes.

Little stars
(*Swedish*)

8 oz. flour	jam
7 oz. iced butter	1 egg, beaten
4 tablesp. iced water	

Sieve the flour on to a pastry board and cut in the butter with a knife
or pastry blender. Gradually add the water, tablespoon at a time and
quickly mix into a ball. Wrap in greaseproof paper and leave in a cold
place for 30 minutes. Roll out on a floured board into a rectangular
shape. Fold into three, seal edges. Cover and chill for 30 minutes.
Repeat this process twice more. Roll out into a square measuring 12
× 12 inches and cut this into nine squares each measuring 4 × 4
inches. Place a little jam in the centre of each square. Cut each corner
1½ inches towards the centre. Fold alternate corners and press point
on to the jam. Chill for 10–15 minutes. Glaze with beaten egg and
cook in a very hot oven (450° F., Gas reg 8) for 8–10 minutes, then
reduce the heat (400° F., Gas reg. 6) and cook for 5–7 minutes.

Macaroons: Ameretti
(*Italian*)

8 oz. ground almonds	3–4 egg whites
12 oz. castor sugar	candied cherries or orange peel
few drops almond essence	

Put the almonds and sugar in a bowl and add the almond essence and
the egg whites. Mix to a fairly stiff paste. (Add 2 teaspoons of water
if needed.) Line a baking sheet with rice paper and drop tablespoons
of the mixture on it. Place a piece of candied fruit on top of every
macaroon and cook in a fairly slow oven (300–325° F., Gas reg. 2–3)
for 25 minutes.

Malaya layer cake: Spiku
(*Malaysian*)

6 eggs	cinnamon
the weight of eggs in sugar	nutmeg
6 heaped tablesp. flour	butter
6 dessertsp. melted butter	

Separate the egg yolks from the whites. Cream the yolks and sugar in
a bowl until light and fluffy. In a separate bowl whisk the egg whites
until stiff. In another bowl put 1 dessertspoon melted butter, 2
tablespoons egg yolk mixture, ¼ teaspoon each of nutmeg and cinnamon. Mix all together and add 2 tablespoons of the whipped egg white.
Fold in remainder. Grease a 7-inch sandwich tin and pour in the mixture. Cook in a moderate oven for 10–12 minutes. Continue this until

all the batter has been finished. When the layers are cool, put them on top of one another and serve.

Mazurek Czekoladowy
(*Polish: Traditional Easter Cake*)

10 oz. flour	*For the icing:*
8 oz. butter	6 oz. unsalted butter
2 oz. castor sugar	2 egg yolks
3 egg yolks, hard-boiled	6 oz. icing sugar
8 oz. almonds, shredded	4 oz. melted chocolate
8 oz. icing sugar	1 liqueur glass brandy
6–8 tablesp. thick cream	
1 lemon (grated rind and juice)	
jam (not very sweet)	

Sift the flour on to a pastry board and chop the butter into it with a knife. Sieve the egg yolks and add them to the flour together with the sugar and lemon rind, and knead quickly into a firm dough. Leave to cool for 30 minutes. Grease a shallow oblong or square tin. Roll out the pastry to ¼-inch thick and line the tin with it. Cook in a pre-heated oven (400° F., Gas reg. 6) until golden in colour. Cool and slip carefully onto a board. Handle the pastry carefully so that it does not break. Mix the shredded almonds, icing sugar, cream and lemon juice together to form a paste. Spread on the baked pastry and cover with jam. Ice with chocolate icing.

To prepare the icing: Cream the butter in a bowl until light and fluffy. Add the egg yolks and sugar and continue beating until well blended. Add the melted chocolate and brandy and mix well.

Pear tart Provençal: Flan aux poires Provençal
(*French*)

For flan:	*For filling:*
8 oz. flour	3 oz. butter
4 oz. butter	3 oz. sugar
2 egg yolks	3 oz. ground almonds
pinch salt	2 eggs
½ oz. castor sugar	1 tablesp. flour
	vanilla essence
For decoration:	
apricot jam	1 tin pears in syrup or equiva-
almonds	lent poached fresh pears

To prepare the flan: Mix the flour, butter, salt, egg yolks and sugar together in a bowl. Knead well. Roll out on a floured board to a thickness of ½ inch. Grease a flan ring and line it with the pastry. Prick the pastry with a fork to prevent it rising. Fill the case with the almond paste and pears arranged in the shape of flowers, and bake in a pre-heated oven (375° F., Gas reg. 5) for 30 minutes or until the pastry is cooked. Remove from the oven and spread a little jam over the pears and sprinkle with chopped, blanched almonds.

To prepare filling: Cream butter with sugar in a bowl, add the almonds, flour, eggs and vanilla and mix until there is a smooth paste. Spread this over the flan case.

Sachertorte
(*Austrian*)

4 oz. butter	*For icing:*
8 oz. castor sugar	2½ oz. castor sugar
4 oz. melted chocolate	½ cup water
grated rind of 1 lemon	2 oz. melted chocolate
8 eggs	knob unsalted butter
4 oz. flour	

Cream the butter in a bowl and gradually add the sugar and the lemon rind. Add the egg yolks one by one and then the chocolate. Beat until light and fluffy. Whip the egg whites stiffly and sift the flour. Fold these, alternately, into the egg yolk mixture. Butter a cake tin and pour in the mixture. Cook in a pre-heated oven at 300° F., Gas reg. 2 for 1 hour. Remove from the oven and allow to cool in the tin. When cold, turn out and cover the top with apricot jam and chocolate icing.

To prepare the icing: Melt the chocolate in a bowl over a saucepan of hot water. Put the sugar and water in another saucepan and bring to the boil. Simmer until the syrup leaves a thread as it drops from a spoon. Add this slowly to the melted chocolate. Stir for 1–2 minutes and add the butter. Pour this icing over the cake and serve with whipped cream.

Schaumtorte
(*Austrian*)

4 eggs	3 tablesp. rum diluted with a
4 oz. castor sugar	little sweetened water
4 oz. self-raising flour	raspberry or strawberry jam or
pinch salt	jelly

For meringue:

3 egg whites   4 tablesp. castor sugar

Put the eggs into a bowl and beat until light and fluffy. Place the
bowl over a saucepan of hot water, add the sugar and whisk until mixture is thick. Remove from the heat and continue whisking until the
mixture is cool. Sift the flour with the salt in another bowl. When the
mixture is cold, gradually add the flour and salt. Butter a 7-inch cake
tin and pour in the mixture. Cook in a pre-heated oven (350° F., Gas
reg. 4) for 50 minutes. Remove from the oven and turn out onto a
rack. Let it cool, then make a few holes in the cake with a skewer.
Pour over it the diluted rum. Put the cake in a greased baking tin,
cover with meringue and make a few dents in the meringue. Spread
the meringue over the sides as well as the top. Put in the oven and
cook for 15 minutes at 300° F., Gas reg. 2 or until meringue is set.
Take out and fill the hollows in the meringue with jam or jelly.

To prepare the meringue: Whisk the egg whites until stiff and fold in
the sugar.

Schenkeli
(*Swiss*)

12 oz. flour   2 tablesp. kirsch or rum
pinch salt   2 oz. shredded almonds
3 oz. butter   3 eggs
5 oz. sugar   fat for deep frying
grated rind of 1 lemon

Sift the flour and salt into a bowl and set aside. In another bowl,
cream the butter and sugar and add the lemon rind, kirsch or rum and
shredded almonds. Beat the eggs and stir them into the mixture. Beat
well. Add the flour and almonds slowly. Knead into a dough and
cover. Leave for 1 hour. Heat the fat in a deep frying-pan. Form the
dough into finger-thick rolls and drop them into the hot fat. Fry until
golden in colour. Drain on kitchen paper and sprinkle with sugar.

Snow balls: Schneeballen
(*German*)

¼ pint milk   2 oz. butter
a small stick cinnamon   2 oz. flour
pinch salt   2 eggs
1 teasp. sugar   fat for frying

Put the milk in a saucepan. Add the cinnamon, salt, sugar and butter and bring to the boil. Remove the cinnamon stick. Sift the flour and add this to the milk. Cook, stirring all the time, until the mixture leaves the sides of the pan. Remove from the heat and add the eggs, one by one, beating well after each has been added to the mixture.

In a deep frying-pan heat some fat. Drop spoonfuls of the mixture into the boiling fat (dip the spoon in fat before scooping up the paste). Fry over a high heat to start with, then reduce the heat when the balls begin to colour and cook for about 15 minutes. Drain on kitchen paper and serve hot, sprinkled with vanilla sugar.

Tort Mickiewicza
(*Polish*)

4 oz. butter	*For the cream:*
4 oz. castor sugar	½ cup single cream
4 eggs	2 oz. castor sugar
4 oz. flour	vanilla essence
	3 egg yolks
	4 oz. butter
	2 oz. icing sugar

Cream the butter in a bowl, add the sugar and beat well until light and fluffy, add the egg yolks one at a time, beating well after each has been added. Whip the egg whites stiffly and fold them into the mixture alternately with the sifted flour. Grease and line a 7-inch cake tin and pour in the mixture. Bake in a pre-heated oven 375° F., Gas reg. 5 for 25–30 minutes. Cool on a rack for about 24 hours. Cut in half, fill and decorate with cream.

To prepare the cream: Add the sugar and vanilla to the cream and place in a double boiler over hot water. Gradually add the egg yolks. Cook, stirring all the time, until the mixture thickens. Remove from the heat. Cream the butter with the icing in a bowl and when the mixture is cold, add it to the creamed butter and icing sugar.

Walnut cake: Nusstorte
(*German*)

6 eggs	1 tablesp. cocoa
6 oz. castor sugar	2 tablesp. dried breadcrumbs
6 oz. shredded walnuts	double cream
juice and rind of 1 lemon	

Cream the egg yolks and sugar in a bowl until light and fluffy. Add the shredded walnuts and lemon rind and mix well. Stir in the lemon juice then the cocoa. Whip the egg whites stiffly and fold them into the mixture alternately with the breadcrumbs. Grease a round baking tin and sprinkle with breadcrumbs. Pour in the cake mixture and cook in a pre-heated moderate oven (350° F., Gas reg. 4) for 30–40 minutes. Turn out and cool. When the cake is cool cut in half and fill with whipped cream. Decorate with whipped cream.

Note: The cake can also be cut into three and each layer sandwiched to the next with whipped cream.

Zebra Kuchen
(*German*)

8 oz. unsalted butter	12 oz. thin sweet biscuits
8 oz. icing sugar	3 tablesp. milk
3 egg yolks	3 tablesp. rum or brandy
4 tablesp. strong coffee	blanched almonds

Cream butter and sugar in a bowl and beat until light and fluffy. Add the egg yolks and beat well, then add the coffee, drop by drop, and continue beating until the mixture is well-blended. Line a cake tin with greaseproof paper and spread a thin layer of the coffee mixture on the bottom. Arrange a layer of biscuits over it and sprinkle them with milk mixed with rum or brandy. Continue this until all the coffee mixture and biscuits have been used up, the last layer being of coffee. Leave in a cold place to set. Turn out and decorate with blanched almonds.

CAKES WITH YEAST

Almond crescents
(*Danish*)

8 oz. flour
1 oz. lard or margarine
pinch salt
¾ oz. yeast
2 teasp. castor sugar
5 tablesp. lukewarm milk
1 beaten egg
5 oz. butter

For filling:
4 oz. shredded almonds
4 oz. castor sugar
2 tablesp. double cream
rind of 1 lemon, grated

Sift the flour and salt. Rub the lard or margarine into the flour. Make a hollow in the centre. Cream the yeast with 1 teaspoon of sugar and add the lukewarm milk. Pour this mixture into the centre of the flour, cover the bowl and leave so that the yeast may rise. When the yeast has risen, add the beaten egg and 1 teaspoon of sugar and mix to a soft dough. Knead on a floured board until smooth. Put the dough into a greased plastic bag or cloth and leave it in the refrigerator for 15 minutes. Work the butter into a flat cake. Take the dough from the refrigerator. Put it on a floured board. Roll it out to a 10-inch square. Put the butter in the centre. Fold over the sides of the dough like an envelope and seal. Roll out into an oblong about 15 inches long and fold into three. Place in a plastic bag or cloth and put in the refrigerator for 15 minutes. Repeat this process twice more, then leave the dough for several hours or overnight. Roll it out and cut it into strips 5 inches wide. Cut these strips into triangles. (If you do not wish to do this, roll out the pastry into 10-inches square and cut again into four equal squares and then each square into two triangles.) Put some of the filling at the base of each triangle and roll up, beginning with the wide side. Shape into crescents and place on a baking tin. Cover and leave to rise in a warm place (not too warm because if this is so the fat will run). When the crescents have risen and are puffy (usually after 20–30 minutes), brush them with beaten egg and bake in a pre-heated oven (425° F., Gas reg. 7) for 12–15 minutes. Remove from the oven and whilst hot, glaze with icing.

To prepare the filling: Mix the shredded almonds, sugar and cream and add the grated lemon rind.

Note: For the icing you need to sift some icing sugar in a bowl. Stir with a wooden spoon and add water—add a little at a time—stirring all the time until a smooth coating consistency is obtained. Add flavouring to taste. Spread over the cakes with a knife which has been dipped in hot water.

Baba
(*Polish*)

8 oz. flour
pinch salt
½ oz. yeast
3 oz. sugar
⅓ cup lukewarm milk or single cream

3 egg yolks
3 oz. butter
grated rind of 1 lemon
vanilla essence
2 tablesp. sultanas

Sift the flour and salt into a bowl and make a well in the centre. Pour in the yeast creamed with 1 teaspoon sugar and some of the luke-warmed milk or cream. Cover and leave to rise in a warm place for 20 minutes. When the yeast has risen, add the egg yolks creamed with sugar, the lemon rind and vanilla and beat well with a wooden spoon or mix in an electric mixer, using a dough hook, until the mixture is well blended and little bubbles appear on the dough. Gradually add the melted butter and continue beating. Add the sultanas and mix well.

Butter generously a fluted 'baba' mould and three-quarters fill it with the dough. Leave in a warm place to rise and when the dough has risen to the top, put in a pre-heated oven at 350° F., Gas reg. 4 for 40 minutes. When cooked, take out of the oven, cool a little and turn out on a rack. Dust the baba with icing sugar, or ice with rum icing or maraschino icing.

Note: If you ice the baba with rum or maraschino, you need to put 5 oz. icing sugar in a bowl, add a few drops of lemon juice and 1 dessertspoon of either rum or maraschino and sufficient water to make a thick syrup.

Baba with rum: Baba au rhum
(*French*)

8 oz. flour
pinch salt
½ oz. yeast
2 tablesp. castor sugar
¼ cup lukewarm milk
2½ oz. butter
1 whole egg
1 egg yolk
dried breadcrumbs

For syrup:
4 oz. castor sugar
½ cup water
4 tablesp. rum

Sift the flour and salt into a bowl and make a hollow in the centre. Cream the yeast with 1 teaspoon of sugar and add the lukewarm milk and pour this mixture into the centre of the flour. Sprinkle a little of the flour on top of the yeast, cover with a cloth and leave to rise in a warm place. When the yeast has risen (after approximately 15–20 minutes) add the rest of the sugar, the beaten egg yolk and the egg. Beat well for a few minutes and add the softened butter, piece by piece. Continue beating until the dough is of a 'dropping' consistency. Grease a well-fluted 'baba' mould, sprinkle with breadcrumbs and fill the mould about three-quarters full with the mixture. Leave to rise to the top of the mould. Bake in a pre-heated oven at 350° F., Gas reg. 4 for 30–40 minutes. Turn out on a rack and pour over the rum syrup. *To prepare the syrup:* Boil the sugar with the water in a saucepan until it forms a syrup. Remove from the heat, wait until the bubbles subside and add the rum.

Dough wreath: Hefenkranz
(*German*)

1 lb. flour
pinch salt
1 oz. yeast
¼ pint warm milk
2 oz. castor sugar
2 eggs
4 oz. butter

For filling:
1 oz. softened butter
3 oz. sultanas
1 oz. candied orange peel
3 oz. castor sugar
¼ teasp. cinnamon

glacé icing

Sieve flour and salt into a bowl. Make a hollow in the flour and pour into it the yeast creamed with 1 teaspoon sugar and a little of the warm milk. Sprinkle a little of the flour on top, cover the bowl and leave in a warm place to rise. Beat eggs and remaining sugar together and soften the butter. When the yeast has risen, add the beaten eggs, the rest of the milk, and beat well. Gradually add the softened butter and beat or knead until elastic. Cover the dough and set to rise to double its size. Turn onto a floured board, knead well and roll into an oblong (about 9 × 18 inches). Spread this with the softened butter and sprinkle with sultanas, candied peel and cinnamon. Roll up from the wide side and press the edges firmly together. Put on a greased baking sheet and form into a ring, joining ends together. Cover and prove for about 30–40 minutes. Bake in a hot oven (425° F., Gas reg. 7) for about 10 minutes, then reduce the heat to 350° F., Gas reg. 4 and bake for further 30 minutes.

When cold coat with icing.

Kumas
(*Indian*)

3 oz. butter or ghee	4 oz. semolina
3 tablesp. sugar	1½ oz. flour
½ oz. yeast	1 oz. shredded almonds
3 tablesp. lukewarm milk	1 teasp. vanilla essence
2 eggs	3–4 cardamoms, ground
1 egg yolk	

Cream together the butter or ghee with the sugar in a bowl. In another bowl, cream the yeast with 1 teaspoon sugar and 1 tablespoon of the milk. Cover and leave to rise for 15 minutes. Add the eggs and the egg yolk, one at a time, to the creamed butter and sugar and beat well. Add the yeast and the rest of the milk. Sift the flour and semolina into a bowl and gradually stir this into the egg mixture. Continue beating until the mixture is well-blended. Add the shredded almonds, vanilla and cardamoms. Grease a shallow tin, 8-inches square, and pour in the cake mixture. Cover and leave to rise in a warm place. When the cake has risen to the top of the tin, place in a pre-heated oven at 350° F., Gas reg. 4 and cook for 30–35 minutes. Leave the cake to cool in the tin, and cut into squares.

Note: I improve the original recipe, given above, by covering the cake with pastry crumble before leaving it to rise in the cake tin. For pastry crumble see 'Yeast cakes', page 242.

Poppy seed cake: Makownik
(*Polish*)

8 oz. poppy seeds	2 oz. orange peel, sliced thinly
4 oz. butter	1 egg
4 oz. sugar	12 oz. flour
6 oz. castor sugar	pinch salt
2 tablesp. thick cream	¾ oz. yeast
1 packet vanilla or	¼ pint lukewarm milk
1 teasp. vanilla essence	2 egg yolks
2 oz. sultanas	granted rind of 1 lemon

Put the poppy seeds into a bowl, pour over them scalding water and leave to soak overnight. Drain and pass through a mincer several times or put in the liquidizer. The poppy seeds should be well-creamed. Melt some butter in a pan, add the poppy seeds and 4 oz. sugar and cook slowly for 1–2 minutes, stirring all the time, add the vanilla and cream and continue cooking slowly and stirring until all the liquid has been absorbed. Add the sultanas and orange peel. Allow the mixture to cool slightly and when it is cooled add a beaten egg. Mix well.

Sift the flour and salt into a bowl. Cream the yeast with 1 teaspoon of sugar and add the milk. Make a hollow in the centre of the flour and pour in the yeast mixture. Sprinkle a little of the flour from the sides of the bowl over the yeast mixture, cover with a cloth and leave in a warm place for 15–20 minutes to allow the yeast to rise. Add the rest of the sugar, the beaten egg yolks and the lemon rind. Beat or knead well, gradually adding the rest of the butter which has been melted. Continue kneading until the dough is smooth and elastic. Cover and leave until it has doubled its bulk. Knead again and roll out into an oblong. Spread the lukewarm poppy seeds mixture on the dough. Roll up. Place in a buttered and floured baking tin and leave in a warm place for 20 minutes. Bake in a pre-heated oven at 425° F., Gas reg. 7 for 5 minutes and then reducing the heat to 350° F., Gas reg. 4 for 25 minutes.

Q

Yeast cakes: Vatrushki
(*Russian*)

8 oz. flour
pinch salt
½ oz. yeast
¼ cup milk
2 teasp. sugar
2 eggs
1 egg yolk
2 oz. butter, melted
grated rind of 1 lemon
vanilla essence
gooseberry jam

For the pastry crumbs:
2 oz. flour
2 oz. butter
1½ oz. sugar

Sift the flour and salt into a bowl and make a hollow in the centre. Cream the yeast with 1 teaspoon of sugar and add the lukewarm milk. Pour this mixture in the centre of the flour, sprinkle a little flour on top, cover with a cloth and leave in a warm place for 15–20 minutes to rise. When the yeast has risen, add the egg yolk and 1 egg beaten with 1 teaspoon sugar. Mix well and knead into a soft dough which does not stick to the sides of the bowl. When the dough is smooth and little bubbles appear on the surface, begin to add the melted butter, beating well all the time. Add the lemon rind and the vanilla and knead until the dough has absorbed all the fat (a little more flour can be added, if needed). Cover the bowl with a cloth and leave to rise in a warm place until the dough has doubled its bulk. Roll out on a floured board to 1-inch thickness, then cut into rounds about 2½ inches in diameter. Grease a baking sheet and place the rounds on it. Cover and leave to rise. With a wine glass or a small pastry cutter make a deep dent in the centre, leaving an inch-wide circle around it. Put a little jam in the centre and sprinkle with pastry crumbs, pressing them down lightly. Brush the circle with beaten egg and bake in a pre-heated moderately hot oven (375° F., Gas reg. 5) for 25–30 minutes.

To prepare the crumble: Blend all ingredients into a firm dough, then grate it on a very coarse grater.

Note: These cakes are excellent filled with curd cheese instead of jam. To make the curd cheese, cream ½ oz. butter with 1 oz. castor sugar. Add an egg yolk and stir in 6 oz. curd cheese. Add the vanilla and mix well.

Rice cake
Sauerkraut
Snow balls
Walnut cake
Whipped sour cream
Zebra Kuchen

Greek
Greek fish
Moussaka

Gujurati, see also *Indian*
Mixed vegetables

Hungarian
Balaton carp
Cheese cake
Debrecen pork chops
Dough crumbs
Eggs scrambled Santelli
Hungarian pancake gâteau
Mushrooms in sour cream
Pork cutlets kolozsvar
Potato paprikash
Sirloin, braised, à l'Esterhazy
Sirloin, stewed, à la Hortobágy
Tomatoes and green peppers
Veal paprikash
Wooden platter steak

Indian
Aubergine pilau
Aubergine salad
Banana balls
Bengali fish curry
Carrot halva
Chicken pilau
Chicken shami kebabs
Chupatties
Egg curry
Eggs, stuffed (p. 56)
Green peppers (stuffed)
Gujurati tomatoes
Ice cream
Kumas
Maize fritters
Masala chops
Masala Dosai
Minced meat curry
Mulligatawny soup
Parathas
Potato balls curry

Prawn and egg curry
Punjabi cauliflower
Puries
Rice, cooking method
Rice dumplings
Rice with chicken
Semolina patties
Spice omelette

Indonesian
Beef rendang
Chicken and vegetable curry
Egg sambal goreng
Java sambal goreng
Mixed salad

Iraqi
Baghdad pilau
Chicken puffs
Iraqi pudding

Israeli
Cottage cheese fritters
Egg and aubergine
Honey cake
Matzo dumplings
Stuffed tomatoes (Agvaniot
    Memulaim, p. 35)

Italian
Biscuit tortoni
Calzone
Cheese (dessert) omelettes
Cheese patties (fried)
Chicken breasts
Cream of celery soup
Eggs with potatoes
Fillet steak with Madeira
Gnocchi, Roman style
Green pepper salad
Macaroons
Meat balls (Polpette, p. 108)
Minestrone soup
Mixed grill
Pasta al forno alla Romana
Pasta with cream
Risotto Milanesi
Spaghetti with peas
Stuffed tomatoes (Pomidori
    ripieni, p. 35)
Veal cutlets Bolognese
Veal kidneys

Duck with red cabbage
Eggs, stuffed (p. 30)
Eggs surprise
Fish with horseradish
Fish with mushrooms
Herrings in sour cream
Mazurek Czekoladowy (cake)
Meat in cabbage leaves
Minced chicken cutlets
Mushrooms with potatoes
Pancakes stuffed with mushrooms
Pig's foot jelly
Polish shortbread with jam
Poppy seed cake
Pork cutlets (p. 93)
Potato dumplings, *also:*
Raw potato dumplings
Ravioli with mushrooms
Red cabbage
Red cabbage salad
Rissoles stuffed with mushrooms
Sour milk pancakes
Spring chickens
Stuffed potato dumplings
Tort Mickiewicza

Portuguese
Fish with vegetables

Punjabi, see also *Indian*
Aubergines, mashed
Biscuits
Chicken tandoori
Rice pudding
Stuffed marrows

Rumanian
Aubergine salad (p. 188)
Meat sausage
Transylvanian beans

Russian
Beef Stroganoff
Bliny
Cheese pancakes
Chicken à la Kiev
Chicken pie
Fish pie
Fruit jelly (p. 198)
Meat balls (Bitochki, p. 107)
Meat pasty

Omelette with caviar
Pascha
Potatoes in sour cream
Sauerkraut soup
Sauerkraut with salted cucumbers
Smoked salmon cornets
Yeast cakes (p. 241)

Scandinavian
Ham rolls
Scandinavian herrings

Serbian
Cauliflower with ham
Maize meal

Siamese
Fishballs and mushroom soup
Kaeng Masaman
Thai noodle soup

Singhalese
Aubergines in coconut milk

Slovakian
Bread dumplings

Slovenian
Macaroni

Spanish
Cold soup (gazpacho)
Egg soup
Fricco
Potato omelette
Spanish rice

Swedish
Little stars (cakes)

Swiss
Apple charlotte
Apple crumble
Butter cakes
Calf's brain soup
Cheese croquettes
Cheese on skewers
Chicory (stuffed)
Eggs à la Suisse

B. General index

Note: English names only are given, unless the name borne by dish in country of origin is so well known abroad that it will be sought for under that name

Sukiyaki, 73, 83
Sweet and sour fish, 71
Sweet and sour sauces: for fish, 71; for meat balls, 108
Sweet yellow rice (cold dessert), 193, 203
Syrup for rum babas, 239

Tamarind juice, use of, 16
Tartare sauce, for fish, 69
Thai noodles soup, 37, 48
Thyme, 16
Toffee apples, 193, 204
Tomato sauce, for stuffed eggs, 56
Tomatoes and green peppers, 169, 187
Tomatoes, Gujurati, 169, 186
Tomatoes, stuffed (Israeli and Italian), 20, 35
Tort Mickiewicza (cream-filled cake), 217, 235
Transylvanian beans (style for French beans), 169, 187
Trout in wine, 59, 71
Turmeric, 16
Turnips served with duck, 166–7

Uncooked coffee cake, 217, 236

Vanilla icing, for Cake from Provence, 225–6
Veal cutlets à la Périgueux, 74, 95
Veal cutlets Bolognese, 74, 97
Veal escalopes: Austrian, Swiss, 74, 97

Veal in white sauce, 74, 99
Veal kidneys, 73, 89
Veal, Lithuanian roast, 74, 96
Veal paprikash, 74, 98
Veal 'sparrows', 74, 98
Vegetable base for fried noodles, 129
Vegetable broth, 49
Vegetable dishes, 169, 171–87
Vegetable soup, 45
Vegetables, mixed: German, 169, 177; Gujurati, 169, 177
Vermicelli (hot dessert), 193, 214
Ve-tsin, 16
Vichyssoise (soup), 37, 49
Viennese nockerl, 193, 215
Viennese roast pork, 74, 94
Viennese soufflé, 193, 215

Walnut cake, 217, 235
Weights, with metric equivalents, 11
White rice, 120, 149
White sauce for Pasta al forno alla Romana, 137
Whiting, baked, 59, 61
Wiener Schnitzel, 74, 97
Wine, in European and Chinese dishes, 16

Yeast cakes, Russian, 217, 242; see also Cakes with yeast, 237–42

Zebra Kuchen (uncooked coffee cake), 217, 236